REPORT FROM NO. 24

REPORT FROM #24

Gunnar Sonsteby

Prepared from a translation from
the Norwegian by Maurice Michael

New York

Published by Barricade Books Inc.
Fort Lee, NJ 07024

www.barricadebooks.com

Library of Congress Cataloging-in-Publication Data
Sonsteby. Gunnar
[Rapport fra nr. 24. English]
Report from no. 24 / Gunnar Sonsteby; [prepared from a translation
from the Norwegian by Maurice Michael].
p. cm.
Originally published: New York: L.Stuart, 1965. With new photos.
ISBN 1-56980-141-X
1. Sonsteby, Gunnar. 2. World War, 1939-1945--Underground movements--
Norway. 3. World War, 1939-1945 Personal narratives, Norwegian.
4. Great Britian. Special Operations executive. Kompani Linge--Biography.
5. World War, 1939-1945--Campaigns--Norway.
6. Soldiers--Norway Biography.
7. Norway--History--German occupation, 1940-1945. I. Title
D802.N8S6613 1999
940.53'481'092--dc21

ISBN: 978-1-56980-812-2 (2017)

20 19 18 17 16 15

Manufactured in the United States of America

Preface

While in command of United States special operations forces some years ago, I had the authority to present the US Special Operations Command (USSOCOM) Medal to persons who merited it through outstanding support of the Special Forces community. The Medal had been presented by my predecessors a few times in the last fourteen years. As I reviewed the list of prior recipients, I realized that all were United States citizens and immediately decided to include a member of the global community of commandos upon which we had come to depend in so many places. We conducted thorough research in order to discover a non-American who was unarguably deserving of the first such medal to be presented to a foreigner. After a couple of weeks, a Lieutenant Colonel brought me a book, *Report From #24*, and said, "*I think we have found the right person.*"

As I read the book, I was struck by Gunnar Sønsteby's selfless dedication, careful planning, disciplined execution and admirable success in so many important missions that we would now describe as "special operations." The physical hardships that he endured, the risks that he took, the losses that he suffered, and the extraordinary personal heroism that he demonstrated were essential elements of his story, which gripped me as few other books had. But mostly, it was the manner of the telling — unemotional, straightforward, appropriately detailed, more like a thrilling documentary than a personal memoir — that impressed me the most. I saw in Captain Gunnar Sønsteby the selfless commitment, the cleverness, the stamina and courage, the honesty and humility that I believe epitomize the best of special operations forces. I agreed that we had found our man.

And, as a 90 year-old three-time recipient of Norway's highest award for wartime valor, Gunnar was certainly a selectee that no one could reasonably challenge.

The Chief of Defense of Norwegian Armed Forces, General Diesen, arranged an award ceremony in Oslo. I was advised on arrival that this would all be a surprise for Gunnar, who had simply been invited to attend a reception. As I began to speak about the symbolic importance of the first foreign presentation of the Medal, it slowly dawned on Gunnar that it was for him, and he appeared genuinely surprised, humbled and a little embarrassed. As I hung the pendant around his neck, he leaned to whisper in my ear, "*Are you sure you've selected the right man?*" I whispered back that, by questioning his selection, he further assured me that we had, in fact, made the right choice.

I am fortunate to have served with many great men and women, but there were only a few times when, after just a short time with someone, I knew for sure that I was in the presence of a highest quality individual. My first meeting with Gunnar was one of those times.

I saw Gunnar a few times after that, both in Norway and the United States as he traveled and lectured throughout his life. He gave my wife and me a personal tour of the Norwegian Resistance Museum at Akershus, where he conducted voluntarily guided tours every week, which I remember in detail mostly because of his unwillingness to talk about his role. I visited the statue of Gunnar and his famous bicycle on Karl Johan Street, near where he first determined that he would dedicate all of his being to ridding Norway of Nazi occupation. My respect for him grew immensely over time, and his death in 2012 struck me and millions of others as a deep and meaningful loss.

Captain Gunnar Sønsteby was indeed a great and important man, and one whose personal story ought to be told again and again. Through this reprinting, we now view another opportunity to immerse ourselves in it. We should be thankful.

—Admiral Eric T. Olson, U.S. Navy, retired
Previous Commander USSOCOM

Introduction

It is most unusual for a book publisher to write a new introduction to a book he originally published more than thirty years ago but this is an unusual book and Gunnar Sonsteby is an unusual man.

I'll never forget the day I first saw him.

My wife Mary Louise and I were in Oslo, Norway, meeting with Finn Jerstad, an executive with one of Norway's largest publishing houses.

The three of us were having lunch in the modernistic glass-enclosed Kon Tiki Restaurant which was built next to the legendary Kon Tiki boat.

In the middle of our conversation, I suddenly felt a wave sweeping through the restaurant of what I can only describe as human electricity. It was obvious that something was happening in the restaurant.

"What's going on?" I asked our host.

Finn replied, "There's Sonsteby and two of his men."

At that point I saw three men walking through the restaurant across from where we were sitting.

"Who's Sonsteby?" I asked.

"He's the author of Norway's #1 best-selling book," Finn Jerstad replied. "He's legendary."

I was fascinated and I quickly bought American book publishing rights.

After an English translation was made, we published *Report from No. 24.*

We got to know Gunnar Sonsteby personally when we brought him to the United States to promote his book and I developed great admiration and affection for him.

In Report from No. 24 he tells his own story and it's one that exceeds any James Bond thriller for excitement.

And every word of it is true!

Report from No. 24 was successful but after several years, it went out of print. American publishing rights were returned to him by my old company.

Last year he visited New York City and it was then that I persuaded Gunnar to allow Barricade Books, my new company, to publish Report from No. 24 again.

This time it would include photographs.

The Germans invaded Norway and Denmark on April 9, 1940 and Scandinavia was now officially involved in World War II.

Sweden continued to remain neutral while Finland fought on the side of the Germans.

There were many proud Danes and courageous Norwegians unwilling to accept occupation. And so a resistance sprang up in both countries.

There are few real heroes in wartime. Gunnar Sonsteby proved himself to be one of these. He showed incredible courage, daring and a determination to resist Nazi oppression at a constant risk to his own life.

Now read the words of the most highly decorated hero of the Norwegian resistance.

Lyle Stuart
New York City
July, 1999

Contents

CHAPTER I

The Beginning

I lay flat on the grass, pistol in hand. The ticking of my wristwatch was matched by the pounding of my heart. For an eternal second I could see the faces of friends who had died at the hands of the Nazis. Three minutes more and the bombs would explode. If we had done our job right, another factory—vital to the Nazis—would be destroyed. Two minutes more. I found myself remembering how I'd gotten here . . . how it all began. One minute. I bit my lower lip. Even if the sabotage was successful, before the evening was over we might all be dead.

The things that nearly happen! I was within an ace of landing a job in Germany about six months before the Germans invaded Norway in 1940. I had received my diploma the year before. Then I applied for a position in a firm of shipowners and brokers in Lübeck, and got the job. A short while later I received a second letter—this one telling me the company had had to make other arrangements.

Thus it was sheer chance that I was not working in Germany when war broke out. Instead, I had found a job in a motor-bicycle shop in Oslo and registered to study economics at the University. I became a regular visitor to the hut the University Athletic Association owned in a glorious stretch of hill and forest at the very door of Oslo. There I became acquainted with many of the young men who became leaders of the Home Front during the German occupation years. I met Knut Moyen, who had nearly beaten all the country's best skiers at the races at Birkebein some years before and was now president of the Student Athletic Society. There, too, I met Per Morland, who was to play a vital role in the Norwegian resistance. He was studying law, but he preferred the hills and forest; and was sometimes out at the hut for two or three days in the middle of the week. He was a bit of an introvert and had little to say. Just sat in his corner, puffing at a pipe and drinking cold black coffee.

At school I had always preferred companions who liked to spend their free time in the open air. For us the mountainous world of Rjukan, a hundred miles west of Oslo, was a paradise, and we were out skiing or tramping almost every weekend and holiday.

The outbreak of war in the heart of Europe in autumn 1939, soon cost me my job in the bicycle shop. It became impossible to import motor bicycles, so no one was needed to sell them. After that, I took a number of temporary jobs, including one as a restaurant porter. I also worked with a saw, for the war had brought birch-wood back into its own and logs were in great demand.

Even the winter war in Finland—a country with which we had a common frontier—seemed remote. I remember that one day, when I was out with a friend from my home town, we met a girl we had gone to school with. She asked us why we had not volunteered to go help the poor Finns. My friend and I looked at each other. The thought of volunteering seemed pretty crazy. War, we felt, was not for us. There was no doubt though that the war in Finland had sent black clouds to darken the blue of Norway's more than a century of peace and all over the country civilians enrolled for voluntary military training in their spare time. We did so too, up at the students' mountain Hut.

I spent Easter of 1940 at the Hut. There had been plenty of snow all winter; skiing had been good; and I was in top form. I came to know the country north of Oslo like the back of my hand.

I now had a job with a big insurance company and had a room in a flat that my parents (who still lived in Rjukan) had bought in Oslo. The rest of the flat was rented to an engineer and his wife, a very pleasant couple. It was there that I spent the evening of April 8th.

There had been rumor after rumor all day but few of us expected what the following day would bring. Not even at midnight, when we stood looking out over the fjord, seeing flashes and hearing the rumble of guns, did we believe it was anything more than a minor incident. I felt relatively carefree when I finally went home to bed.

I was jolted awake in the morning by an air raid siren. Every radio in the building was switched on, they all blared the unbelievable news that the Germans had invaded Norway and instructed us to take shelter in the basement. My immediate reaction was rebellion. I was appalled and indignant—so much so that, while the others obediently trooped down to the basement, I stayed where I was. No one was going to interrupt my breakfast! I had the right to eat my egg and drink my coffee in peace.

As I walked to the office that morning, there were more "interruptions," and I had to take cover in doorways as planes came flying across the rooftops, machine-guns firing.

At the office we gathered in groups to discuss the situation and talk about our experiences. Then I went out and walked the streets. German guards had sprouted up outside the Head Post Office and steel-helmeted Germans were marching in tight formation down Karl Johan (the main street). Machine-guns had been set up in the park behind the Royal Palace. I gaped at it all, unable to accept the fact that it had really happened, that the King and Government had left Oslo and were now "somewhere in Norway." Everyone I met on that incredible morning seemed just as stupefied as I was.

The next morning there seemed nothing to do but to go to the office as usual—to talk and speculate. Just at lunch time there came a wildfire rumor that the city was going to be bombed and that everyone must get out—out and away as quickly as possible. It was a day of panic, and many people were quick to obey the anonymous order to drop everything and get out of the "doomed" city. Again, my reaction was anger. I was damned if I was going to let anyone disturb my meals, so I sat in the canteen with a cup of chocolate and my sandwiches. I was certain this report that the city was to be bombed and evacuated was only stupid rumor. But there were not many others besides the caretaker and me in the building by the time I had finished my lunch. Outside, even Karl Johan was relatively deserted. When the office closed at the end of the day, I went home and let the world go its very crooked course.

It was not till the next morning, Thursday, that people seemed able to think and, at last, to act. Foreign radio stations now gave us our first reliable reports of the fighting and of the partly successful resistance being put up by our troops. Also, we were told, Allied help was coming. One of the men at the office, Philip Hansteen, was a lieutenant in the reserve. Communications were cut with his depot at Fredrikstad, so he had been unable to rejoin his regiment on mobilization. He now called upon his friends and acquaintances to make their way individually to a hut he had in the hills thirty miles or so north of the city. From there the group would try to make contact with the Norwegian forces as a more or less organized body. A friend and I agreed that there was only one course open for us: to go and fight. But then—and this was typical of how in those early days we failed to adjust to the new situation—there arose the question: Would we be allowed to go? Would the office allow us the time off? I went in to my boss and asked rather cautiously whether I might be allowed to go.

"For Heavens sake, man! Off you go!" was the answer.

The two of us went home to change and get our skis, and that afternoon we were on a train for Grua, thirty miles away. There were other "excursionists" on the train whom we suspected had the same destination. I found that I even knew one or two of them. We exchanged glances, but did not speak to each other.

That evening a dozen or more of us had assembled at Hansteen's hut. Hansteen himself had come on skis from just outside the city in broad daylight, wearing uniform and bandalier, with two Colt pistols and a couple of hundred rounds of ammunition in a rucksack. Before turning in, we patrolled the vicinity of the hut. All was quiet.

We were up at five o'clock the next morning and held a council of war over breakfast. A patrol sent to a farm overlooking the village of Jevnaker, a few miles away, came back with the news that there were Norwegian troops in Jevnaker itself and well to the south as well. With Hansteen as our leader, we went in a body to Brandbu, seventeen miles up Lake Randsfjorden from Jevnaker, where there was a depot which now served as a rallying center. Within twenty-four hours about a thousand men were brought there from the local reporting centers, organized, and sent to the front. All trained skiers were formed into a special company under Hansteen's command.

All this activity had to be camouflaged and was performed under a constant air raid alarm. Big German bombers kept flying low over us, but they dropped no bombs.

Philip Hansteen's ski company consisted of four platoons of thirty men each and a headquarters section of fifteen men. I was in No. 4 platoon. Hansteen's brother, Axel, commanded it. The company was loosely organized so each platoon could operate more or less independently in the territory north of Oslo, watching for movements of enemy troops and preventing civilians from returning to Oslo, because they might give our positions away. That evening fighting was reported at Stryken, on the main Oslo road twenty-five miles to the south, and we were all bundled into lorries and sent there post haste. It proved to be a false alarm, so we withdrew a mile or two to Harestua and crowded into a boarding house for the night. Another false alarm had two hundred of us tumbling out sleepily at half past two in the morning to deal with Germans. The alarm was raised because lights had been seen in the woods, but they turned out to be the lights of evacuees from Oslo who had got themselves lost.

The next day my platoon was sent south to reconnoiter. While we were on reconnaissance, the rest of the company was called back to Grua in a hurry to strengthen the Norwegian forces there. The Germans were on the way.

Philip Hansteen would never retreat. For his excellent work during the next few days, he was promoted to Captain. He was killed at Bjorgeseter on April 17, after the German break-through.

During the retreat northward my platoon commander, Axel Hansteen, was taken prisoner. The rest of us joined another ski company and continued north, always a few miles behind the main force. We continually saw burned farms and blown-up bridges, the latter the act of our withdrawing forces, the former the vengeful work of the Germans. Day after day, we made our laborious way northward. We were short of food and desperate for sleep, for we could never find decent shelter at night. We were badly equipped and not one of us had dry shoes for three weeks.

On the way I acquired a pair of dungarees. I put them on and stuffed my uniform into my rucksack. The result was a bad chill.

At the end of April we were still trailing behind the main forces, having been driven up as far as Ostre Gausdal, twenty miles north of Lillehammer. Then, at the end of April, our dwindling company had to go into action at Svingvold. My chill had developed into bronchitis and sinusitis; in fact it probably had already turned into pneumonia without my realizing it. But they were tragically short of men at Svingvold and, wretched though I felt, I had to help relieve the poor devils who were bearing the brunt of the action. I had not yet learned to respect danger, and in my stupidity I walked across many open spaces when I should have crawled. One of the skiers asked me if my temperature was so high that I was delirious. Perhaps it was.

On May 3 all further organized operations were declared impossible and we were told to go back home. Some of the men decided to go to Rjukan, away to the southwest in Telemark, where there was still said to be fighting. I joined them, for I felt it was too awful just to give in. I realized that I was ill, but I hoped that I was over the worst of it and tracked along after the others. The snow was loose and the going heavy.

Up in the mountains we came across other skiers with the same goal as ours. Otherwise we saw no one in that desolate part of Norway. We pushed on, heading southwest. We sank in snow to our knees during the day, though things got a bit better in the evening when it froze.

I was getting worse and worse. Plagued by thirst, I had to drink from every stream we came to, and regularly I reached the place where we were to spend the night three or four hours after the others. After three days of this, I was pretty well done. We had reached a farm belonging to a member of the company, where we were beautifully looked after; but I felt weary and limp no matter how much I rested. Then we heard that an Oslo businessman who had a hut in the next valley was going to drive down to Oslo. He gave me a lift, and that evening I was back in my room in Oslo. I sent a telegram home to Rjukan—a laconic "All well"—and then collapsed. The wife of the other tenant of the flat had been a nurse and she sent for a doctor, who packed me straight off to the hospital.

It was pneumonia and sinusitis, both acute because of neglect and exposure. They pulled me round and after several weeks I was discharged, but I was told that it would be at least two years before I would entirely recover.

So there I was in German-occupied Oslo. Oh, the humiliation of seeing those green-uniformed creatures tramping our streets, secure and triumphant, masters of the situation. I watched German civilians popping in and out of Norway's Parliament building as though it were the most natural thing in the world! But what pained me the worst was seeing our own Nazi-sympathizers drop their facade of patriotism and raise their traitorous voices. I was depressed and savage, and the only way I could get away from the misery and frustration of it all was to go up to the Students' Hut in the hills north of the city, where I could always find others who shared my feelings.

The first few times I was there, I realized that what I had gone through had set its mark on me. I had acquired a fear of the woods—at least of being alone in the woods. I was determined to conquer this fear and get back on the old terms with the woods and the wilds. I went out for long solitary trips and gradually achieved this.

I had no intention of waiting two years before "complete recovery," so I started training. And I got fit again in an even shorter time than I had hoped.

That summer and autumn the Hut was a rallying point for the patriotic members of the Association. We listened to each other's war experiences, discussed the London news broadcasts—to which we all listened—and more and more we realized that war was still being waged out there in the wide world, while for us it was already over. Or was it? The arms we had buried before we made our way home were still lying where we had hidden them. One thought led to another. Slowly, the idea of a resistance was being born.

CHAPTER II

To and Fro Across the Frontier

For the second time I lost my job because of the war. Like many other companies, my firm had to cut down its staff and I was one of the victims. So I resumed full-time studies, but not for long. Soon I had more important things to do. I had begun to meet people who were engaged in resistance work and it wasn't long before I found myself the same. First, I had a "job" with a clandestine newspaper acting as its equally clandestine paper boy.

The building in Therese Street where I lived extended back to the parallel street and there was a central courtyard between the two frontages which the occupants all shared. In this other part of the building lived three men, Harald Hanto, Max Manus, and Kolbein Lauring, who were engaged in all sorts of resistance work including the secret newspaper *Vi vil oss et Land*. I forget now who put me in touch with them, but they were glad for help, so I began working for them and their group, which included former volunteers who had gone to Finland to help the Finns fight the Russians. My little arsenal had now shrunk to one air pistol, but that was still something and Hanto, Manus, and Lauring used to come up to my room and we would practice with it.

From paper boy I was promoted to reporter, and now one of my tasks was to obtain exact information about the unpleasant affair at the Commercial College, when a detachment of Quisling's undaunted guards had attempted to turn out the students for subversive propaganda. They had brutally assaulted and knocked down not only pupils, but members of the staff and the principal.

Later in the autumn Max Manus and others of his group went to the southwest coast hoping to get a boat and sail across to England. (That had become the great ambition of most of us now.) But they were all back in Oslo before Christmas after a hard and disappointing trip.

Then I got another job—this time in my home town, Rjukan. The job was in the saltpeter factory there, and in the New Year I left Oslo and went back home. It was my first big stroke of luck since war had broken out, for a fortnight later the State Police struck at the group for which I had been working. This was the famous occasion, described in Max Manus' book *Underwater Saboteur*, when he dived straight through the blackout curtain and window, but hurt his back and was arrested after all. He was so badly injured that he had to be taken to the hospital—and he escaped from there.

All that spring in Rjukan I spent as much time as I could in the mountains. There I made tentative contact with the beginnings of Milorg, the military group which was one of the two resistance organizations that together made up the Home Front. These contacts took on a more concrete form when I returned to my old rooms at Therese Street in Oslo in the early summer.

In the first few weeks after my return to Oslo, I had a lot to do with a controversy inside the Student Athletic Association. A collaborator (one of the young men I had met up at the Students' Hut in the summer of 1940) had offered his services to the Norwegian Nazis in running the University Athletic Association. He was appointed secretary, so early in June the legally elected management committee of the hut met and resolved to notify the newly appointed Nazi manager of our Association of our resignation. We duly sent in our letters, and some days later I resigned from the Association altogether.

My job left me fairly independent and though I worked a lot in the evenings, I had little or nothing to do on Saturdays. This was important, as I was now in contact with the Milorg people in Oslo. My contacts were a dentist and a businessman, both trained army officers.

The dentist's chair is an excellent place for imparting and receiving secret information and instructions.

My first job for Milorg was to lay the framework of its organization in Ostlandet, a largish territory extending from Kragerö north to the Dovre mountains and then across to the Swedish frontier. First I went to Fagernes to see some people suggested as likely contacts. They in turn suggested other recruits in other places. And so it went on, rather like a chain letter. In a short time I had recruited several schoolmasters (one of whom became a general), a number of policemen, a solicitor, a docker, etc.

Our rendezvous in Oslo was a restaurant in St. Olavs Place, Gildevangen. Here we could meet as though by chance, and here I usually received my instructions. One of our tasks was to dig up the arms that had been hidden away at the end of the fighting in 1940. We eventually collected a good number of rifles. I was going to the Students' Hut again, and I introduced my friend Knut Haugland from Rjukan to the hut. Haugland was a radio telegrapher, trained in the Engineers, and he and Moyen and some others concocted a great plan for building a transmitter so that we could communicate with England.

On odd occasions that summer, Haugland stayed in my room at Therese Street. One day the State Police came up to the flat with him. I wasn't at home. The police poked about and found all his radio material; fortunately Haugland was employed at a radio factory and had a plausible excuse for such things in his room—plausible enough at any rate for the police not to arrest him then and there. Although he seemed to have got away with it, it was thought best that he should go into hiding. I can't help laughing when I remember what awful amateurs we were in those days. Haugland's method of going into hiding was to live in a tent, which he pitched on the hillside just above a lake within two miles of the city! Then he decided to go to Sweden and try to get to England from there.

I had gradually got to know several of the chiefs of the military organization, and I even met the great chief of Milorg, Haneborg Hansen, in person. This meeting took place in the office of a goldsmith. The walls were lined with safes and I can still see the Major fingering through the papers I had brought, hands cased in the black gloves that he affected because it was all so hush-hush and he mustn't leave his fingerprints anywhere. I thought such behavior dreadfully exaggerated. If one was arrested by the Gestapo, it was for quite different reasons than a fingerprint on a piece of paper. The usual reason for a resistance worker being arrested was that another had been arrested in the street or by chance, while carrying a paper with names on it, or else had been tortured and compelled to disclose the names of those he worked with. This exaggerated attention to security coupled with a lamentable lack of action made me lose patience with Milorg.

It seemed to me that we were getting nowhere. More and more I wanted to get to England. Haugland and I had been put into contact with one of the managers of the Esso Petroleum Company, Fridtjof Hoyer, and he was trying to get Haugland and some other radio telegraphers into a tramp steamer in the coastal traffic. The idea was that when the steamer got to Haugesund on the west coast, they could desert and make their way to England. Nothing had come of this, however, and Haugland was impatient to get away as soon as he could. Then someone put us in touch with an antique shop owner in Oslo who had become an "exporter" of refugees as a sideline, and he agreed to export us.

On October 12, Haugland and I left Oslo. Our "exporter" had arranged for us to go to Halden, which is only sixteen miles from the Swedish frontier. At Halden, we went to the taxi stand and asked for a driver named Sandberg. He drove us to the Norwegian customs station at Bokerod, north of the road to Ed, where we were to see Johan Ostlie, one of the customs officers. We reached Bokerod late on the evening of October 12. Ostlie and his family could not have been kinder. Ostlie himself was an ordinary-looking man. I suppose you would say that he was typically Norwegian. Certainly he was a fearless man and in him and his family there was an element of greatness. Bokerod itself was a tiny frontier village with only two or three houses. A small river a few yards away marked the actual boundary line at that time. There was very little traffic through the wooded part of the country, and there were no German guards permanently stationed at Bokerod. The Swedish side was equally sparsely inhabited, so that any stranger attracted attention. In the pitch darkness that night, two of Ostlie's sons took us across the small river and well into Swedish territory.

We had been told to avoid the Swedish guards and make our way to Ed, where we could take a train to Stockholm; but it wasn't long before we ran into a couple of frontier guards. There we were in the Swedish forest, walking along in our best suits, wearing overcoats and soft hats and each carrying a suitcase. That was the get-up recommended to us for inconspicuous travel by train from Oslo to Halden; but being dressed like that in the heart of the forest had the opposite effect. The guards took us to the nearest customs post; from there we were escorted to Ed and so to the reception center for Norwegian refugees up in Smaland, where we were questioned, released, and allowed to proceed to Stockholm.

Being a radio telegrapher, Knut Haugland was welcomed in Stockholm with open arms and was told to be ready to go to England. Having no such skills, I was left to kick up my heels, becoming more and more irritable at nothing to do. Then I heard that it might pay to apply to the British Legation. There I was told that the only means of getting to England was by boat—from Norway; I should go back and try my luck at Alesund, the center for this illegal traffic.

Then I ran into another Norwegian in my plight, Claus Helberg, and we decided to have a shot at it together. What set us on the Alesund route was a news item we heard via a British Legation representative (who worked at the Norwegian Legation) that people were being recruited for a so-called Norwegian Freedom Company in England.

My companion worked out a route for getting to Alesund by train, bicycle, and Shanks' pony. Our presence and activities in Sweden were illegal and to throw a little dust in the Swedes' eyes, we started north on the first stage of our journey. Very early on the morning of October 26 we boarded the train for Sveg. We got into the same compartment but sat at opposite ends of the seat and pretended not to know each other. In fact, we never spoke to anyone, so that people wouldn't know we were Norwegians.

About five o'clock that afternoon, the train pulled into the little town of Sveg, 320 miles north of Stockholm. We walked outside the town to where Helberg had cached a couple of old bicycles. We waited until dark, then mounted and pedaled westward toward the frontier, heading for Lofsdalen some fifty miles away.

We wore summer-weight suits and thin overcoats. Our rucksacks were anything but fat. We were certainly not prepared for winter weather, but we hadn't gone many miles before we were pedaling along in a real snow storm. It was bitterly cold and for the last dozen miles to Lofsdalen we continually had to carry our bicycles through great drifts. This being a road to the frontier, the Swedes had set up a road block and there was a military post, but we managed to pass through unobserved in the dark.

My bicycle collapsed only 500 yards from the farm that was our immediate objective. Helberg had been to the place before and knew the people. The weather was now appalling. There was already more than a foot of snow and it was freezing hard. It was six in the morning by the time we reached the farm, so we dared not linger. We rested for an hour and set off on our next stage, which consisted of some forty to fifty miles across country to the tourist hut at Svukuriset above Lake Femund, our first objective in Norway. The people at the farm offered to lend us skis, but we felt that they wouldn't be any help on the new snow—especially as we would have to cross considerable stretches of moor and bog.

We became very familiar with the bog. All day we trudged along, our feet continually going through the layer of snow into the icy water beneath. I did not have proper boots and my feet were soaked.

At seven o'clock that evening we were still in Sweden. We came to a farm, the only one for miles around. We ought to have sought shelter there for the night, but Helberg did not know the people and was afraid they might report us to the frontier guards. My feet and trouser-legs were sopping, but on we went—for the second night in succession.

We were in very wild country and the going became next to impossible. We were making for a hut on the mountainside of a Lapp who had helped Helberg on a previous journey and was considered reliable.

It became colder and colder. This hardened the snow, but not enough to keep our feet from going through at every step. By midnight we still hadn't found the hut. The temperature had plummetted still further. Our socks, trousers, and shoes were solid ice, and I felt the first symptoms of frostbite, my legs becoming stiffer and stiffer. We struggled across a large scree leading down to a stretch of water. The stiffness had extended to my knees and I knew I would soon be incapable of going further. My companion was pretty well done too. I began to think we were not going to survive our little adventure.

I managed to summon the strength for one more effort but when another half hour's laborious search had got us no further, I gave up. I began shoveling snow aside, intending just to lie down where I was and sleep. Meanwhile, Helberg took another look around to see if he could locate the Lapp's hut, and this time luck was with him. After a few minutes' reconnaissance he found the hut, only 300 yards away. We struggled to it. Fortunately the Lapp was at home and let us in.

It was not far into the night. The first thing I did was put my feet over the fireplace so the ice on my boots would melt and Helberg could pull them off. It took a long time to get the blood circulating again, and the pain in my legs and feet was intense.

The Lapp's hut was built of turf. In the middle of it was a big hearth, and the smoke from the fire went straight up and out through a hole in the roof. The hut was appallingly draughty. and later it became bitterly cold inside. Luckily we induced the Lapp to make up his fire, so at least the part we turned to the hearth was warm.

We had covered nearly half the distance to Svukuriset, with twenty-five miles yet to go. I shuddered at the prospect.

In the morning I was covered with chilblains from toe to knee. I had to cut them open with my knife to get my boots on.

The Lapp lent us a pair of skis with withe bindings, and it was decided that I should use these, while Helberg tried to walk the twelve miles or so that separated us from the next Lapp hut. That march to the second Lapp hut was sheer torment for both of us. We started out at seven o'clock and took several hours to cover the distance. Though my legs hurt, the journey was much easier on skis. The snow was deep, and poor Helberg found the going very difficult. It was not long before I was well ahead of him, but fortunately I found the hut without difficulty. Helberg reached it an hour later. Here we rested, and later in the day moved off again and managed to cover the last dozen miles. Thanks to the skis, I reached the cluster of farm houses at Syllen about six that evening. Helberg was nowhere to be seen. We became desperately anxious, and the farm people went out in search of him. But he turned up about midnight, exhausted.

The next day, we reached the tourist hut at Svukuriset. I could not have gone much further. I was scarcely able to move my legs. From the tourist hut on we got a lift down to Femunds, and from there a boat took us up the thirty-five miles of water to the north end of the lake, where we caught the local bus to Röres on the main railway line.

As we were heading for Alesund, we had to make a cross-country journey involving several changes. The next train in our direction did not leave Röros till five o'clock the next morning, so we had to spend the night in this little town. We didn't feel safe from Germans and Nazis even there, but we took a chance and went to the hotel. We both had the kind of identity cards that were issued in the frontier areas. Helberg's was for Röros district, mine for Halden, which was itself a bit suspicious. Both cards were false. However, we were duly registered at the hotel and given a room.

That night my legs gave me a lot of trouble. All the skin had peeled off and I realized I could neglect them no longer. Helberg had to go to the train alone, while I remained at the hotel.

Later I went to the hospital. The doctor who saw me caught on at once, and I was quickly tucked in bed with my legs anointed and covered with plaster of Paris up to the knee. No one asked for my identity card, national health certificate, or ration card. It was lovely to have proper treatment and I thoroughly enjoyed the sympathy of the nurses, who had been horrified by the look of my legs. The only possible fly in the ointment was the hotel. The people there knew that I had gone to the hospital, but were they all right?

At the end of a fortnight I asked to have the plaster removed from my legs because a boat from England was due at Maloyleia near Alesund on November 13 and I wanted to make a last effort to catch it. The doctor realized what was afoot, and reluctantly he did what I wanted.

I tottered to the station and caught the train to Storen in the northwest. My legs were very sore and I discovered that my toes were beginning to turn dark. By the time I reached the junction at Storen, I knew I had to give up trying to get to England. All the ghastly trip from Stockholm had been in vain.

From Storen I took the next train to Oslo so I could get my legs taken care of.

CHAPTER III

In Prison in Sweden

Back in Oslo my friends got busy and through various channels, including a bookseller, I was put in touch with one of the chief doctors at the Red Cross, and he tackled the business of getting my feet and legs right again. I was very impatient, longing to get to England.

At last, I was pronounced well enough to go and soon was on the train heading north again. I had been given funds for the trip by members of the embryonic resistance movement.

Traveling via Andalnes and Alesund I reached Bryggja without difficulty and began trying to track down the boat. I went to see a local doctor, but received the impression that he felt there was something a bit mysterious about me. At last, I met some of the boys, but they were very down in the mouth, having just made a vain trip to Maloy. The boat from England had never come and no one knew why. Later, we learned that she had been delayed by a violent storm, in which one of the Shetland gang's other boats, the *Blia*, had gone down taking with her forty men from Stavanger district, who were going to England. The boat meant for us eventually reached Maloy but, not finding us, took others instead. Altogether, eight of us from Stockholm had made our way there by devious routes.

The only thing I got out of this long trip was a good map of Maloy, which I subsequently sent to England via Sweden. It proved useful later on.

Back in Oslo, I could think of nothing but getting back to Stockholm to see if there was something I could do for the Norwegian military office there—that is, if they still wouldn't send me to England. In the back of my mind, perhaps, was the idea that all my bad luck would arouse their sympathy and induce them to send me across by plane.

Again I was instructed to go via Halden. On this trip I had two companions. One was an Oslo journalist who had attracted the unwelcome attention of the Germans and had to get out. The other was Per Morland, my friend from the Students' Hut. He, too, was making for Stockholm and England. This time, we reported to the police station in Halden, where the official in charge took us to his home in the actual police building and kept us hidden there till dark. We were driven to Bokerod after dark by the same taximan, Sandberg. At Bokerod, we again sought out customs officer Ostlie, and he and his family saw us safely across the frontier.

I must say a bit more about Ostlie and his family. Johan and Tora Ostlie were my first acquaintance with those heroic people of the frontier district who did so much, risking and often sacrificing their lives and property to help refugees get out of the country safely. Gradually I came to know a lot of them in Halden, Kongsvinger, and in the forests along the frontier, but the Ostlies were the first. They had four children, yet they did all this gladly knowing from the beginning that sooner or later they must be found out. And so they were. Ostlie was arrested at the end of May, 1943, and sent to Grini prison in Oslo. His wife, Tora, and oldest son, Arno, continued the good work. Mrs. Ostlie managed to get through the rest of the war, but Arne was caught in January, 1945.

So, for the second time, I found myself walking in the forest at night. Then we realized that we were safe. The journalist, who had been living on a volcano for some time, bubbled over with high spirits. In fact, we were all so exuberant that we agreed we could sit down and enjoy a breather and a smoke. The journalist could not resist breaking into song and he bellowed away between every puff. Imagine our horror when we walked on a few paces and found ourselves in front of one of those famous notice boards the Germans had set up proclaiming that anyone attempting to cross the frontier would be shot!

Somehow or other we must have crossed back to the Norwegian side without knowing it. We took to our heels and ran east as fast as our legs would carry us.

Eventually we reached the highway on the Swedish side, and followed it till we came to a village. We went to one of the houses, knocked, and asked where the nearest police station was. When they heard we were refugees, they told us to go across to the house of a customs officer a short distance away.

I was unpleasantly surprised when I saw the man. It was the same one who had been in charge of me a month before. I realized this might easily lead to trouble, but hoped the man would not recognize me. He did. He looked at me closely and said:

"But you were here a month ago?"

"No. You must be mistaken."

"What's your name?"

"Gunnar Olsen," I replied without stopping to think.

The man began questioning me further, and grew more and more annoyed as I denied having been in Sweden before. In the end he became quite angry.

This episode had an unfortunate effect on our reception by the Swedes. The customs man rang up his superiors, who reported the matter to the police. Later that morning we were questioned and searched. My Maloy map and various papers were wrapped up in black cloth in my jacket pocket. While the other two were being searched, I was allowed to sit on the old leather sofa. My hat was lying beside me and, while the attention of the police was taken up with the other two I carefully pulled the little package out of my pocket and slipped it under my hat. When my turn came, I walked forward calmly, and all was well.

That afternoon we were sent to Ed. We had the feeling that we were being watched. At Ed we were taken to see the military authorities. There was one captain who tried to pump me and wanted to know everything about the Germans in Norway, especially in the frontier districts. He seemed trustworthy so I told him all I knew, including particulars of conditions I had seen up and down the country.

As time wore on, we were no longer being watched so carefully. We were sent for the night to a boarding house, where there were other refugees from Norway, and the next day the whole lot of us were sent to the Norwegian refugee camp at Öreryd, through which I had already passed a month before. At once I got in contact with the Norwegian military authorities and was allowed to go to Stockholm the following day. There I saw both Norwegian and British officers and reported the failure of the boat to reach Maloy and told them about the men who had been unable to get away because of this.

I did not enjoy Stockholm. I had to rely on my own resources and had no proper papers; fortunately I had plenty of money. Then the British in Stockholm gave me an assignment: I was to go back to Oslo to try to find out certain things for them, especially all I could about the new U-boat harbor the Germans were building at Trondheim. I hoped this time, I could follow an easier route than the one Helberg and I had used. The Norwegian Military Officer gave me a route through Arvika and Kongsvinger to Oslo and my journey was uneventful. Back in Oslo, I got in touch with my old friends and again installed myself in my parents' flat in Therese Street, where I let it be understood that I had been staying in the country.

Through my friends I learned that all radio communication was cut off with England and I was asked to go back to Stockholm for money and parts needed to get the transmitter working again. I agreed to do this. Just before I left, I had a narrow squeak. I ran into a former contact, the man from Esso who had tried to help my friend Haugland get to England. The Esso man wanted me to meet one of his contacts, a lawyer, and we arranged to meet at the man's office some days later. A day or two before our meeting date the Esso man went to the lawyer's office and found both the Germans and the State Police there in possession. The poor Esso man was beaten up and spent three weeks under interrogation. Again I was lucky, for I was warned in time that the lawyer had been arrested so I never went near his office.

I had decided to go back to Stockholm a few days before Christmas. I was doubtful as to the best route, but finally took the advice of some new contacts and headed for Kongsvinger, where I could get help from Sverre Herdal. There was no special check on those traveling by train to Kongsvinger, although it would have attracted attention if one had worn ski clothes and at the same time carried a lot of baggage. I reached Kongsvinger in the afternoon. It was already dark, and I had difficulty in finding my way to Herdal's address. At one point I was stopped by a German in uniform, who asked to see my identity card. I replied that I lived in Kongsvinger and did not have the card on me. He accepted that.

I found Herdal at home and, luckily for me, he decided to take a chance on this unknown person who came with greetings from a mutual friend, and let me stay the night. The next morning Herdal told me that one of the local taxi drivers would probably be able to help me on my way. As it happened, the man was engaged to drive the district doctor on a round of visits up by the frontier, so he suggested that I go with him as a sort of helper. He had a wood-gas generator which required re-charging and re-fueling every now and again, and I could do this for him. So I spent a pleasant day driving around with the doctor and, when the visits had all been made, I was driven to a lake almost on the frontier.

I had the name of a farmer who lived within two or three hundred yards of the frontier who had already helped a number of our couriers across. From him I received instructions on how to get through the Swedish customs station and down to Mitandersfors, where I would be able to catch a bus. There was one due to leave at six-thirty in the morning. The snow lay very deep in the woods and the going might be difficult. The farmer reckoned that it would take me nearly three hours to get to Mitandersfors, so it was arranged that I should start from the farm at half past three.

That evening I went down to the cowhouse with its four or five cows, and I noticed an old wind breaker hanging there. That gave me an idea and I asked the farmer if he would trade it for my relatively new jacket. He thought this an excellent deal and so we made the swap. Before I left I made a paper parcel of my pyjamas, underclothes, and toilet things which I could tuck under my arm, and left my rucksack at the farm. I later learned that the farmer had continued to help couriers across the border until January 1942, when one of his neighbors informed on him and he was arrested by the Gestapo.

It was nearly four o'clock when I set out. The night was dark and rather cold. I walked off on the route I had been given, but was soon floundering in snow up to my middle and having a hard time of it. The worst was that I found great difficulty in keeping my directions. After a while I realized I was not going to do what I had planned for I had already been scrambling around in the woods for a couple of hours.

The only thing to do was to follow my tracks back to the highway and use that.

It was nearly five-thirty when I reached the highway again, emerging just beside the gate across it at the Swedish customs station. All was quiet and peaceful, so I took a chance, ducked under the gate, and walked on into Sweden. There wasn't a soul to be seen anywhere.

A few minutes later I saw a Swedish sentry. I went on up to him, called out a Swedish "Hey!" and received a cheery "hey!" in return. He made no attempt to stop me. I felt considerably safer now and reached the bus station just before six-thirty.

With my paper parcel tucked under my arm, I boarded the waiting bus. Unfortunately my wind breaker stank so strongly of cowhouse that those in the seats nearest to me were forced to move away. Otherwise the trip to Arvika, forty miles to the south, was uneventful, as was my journey to Stockholm by train.

In Stockholm I went to the British and Norwegian authorities and made my reports, and then to Uppsala for Christmas. I had several friends among the Norwegian refugees studying at Uppsala, while awaiting their turn to be sent to England, and we celebrated Christmas together.

Shortly after Christmas I heard that the Swedish police were looking for me. Being a "wanted" person, I thought it safest to go back to Stockholm, but when I got there neither the British nor the Norwegians could give me anywhere to live, because I had no papers of any kind. I had to look after myself as best I could, and again I was lucky. The proprietress of a certain pension was very pro-Norwegian and took the risk of housing me and one or two others in the same precarious situation.

When I wasn't conferring with the British, I spent my time in various cafes drinking coffee. I thought it better not to be in the pension during the day. Then, it was decided that I was to go back to Oslo with money and instructions to enable radio communications with England to be resumed.

I left Stockholm on January 9, 1942, and traveled back the way I had come—westward to Arvika. In my suitcase I had 8,500 Crowns in Norwegian notes for the radio people in Oslo. As before, I had a number of missions and assignments, some of them for the Norwegian Legation.

I dared not travel right through to Arvika for fear of attracting unwelcome attention, and got a ticket to Laxa, a junction a good distance from the frontier. I felt that in Laxa I could safely buy a second ticket to Arvika, without anyone thinking anything of it. My intention was to walk from Arvika to Mitanderfors and so across to Kongsvinger and Oslo, the way I had come. However, my train was late and when it reached Laxa I had no time to buy another ticket, but had to run across and jump into the Arvika train. I could scarcely hope that the ticket collector would not notice my Norwegian accent. The collector, an elderly man, soon appeared and I asked for a ticket to Arvika.

"Are you Norwegian?" he asked.

"No, I'm not," I replied in my best Swedish.

"Yes, you are. Where are you going?"

"To Arvika."

"Where do you live in Arvika?"

I named a street, saying the first thing that came into my head, and the man peered at me suspiciously, but he wrote me out a ticket nonetheless.

As the train stopped in Karlstad East station, I saw the ticket inspector step down onto the platform and say something to a man standing there and pointing towards the compartment where I was sitting. I realized that I was in for trouble and, as the train moved off, I went to the men's room and tore my Norwegian identity card and other papers with my name on them into tiny pieces and washed them down the shaft. A minute or two later we stopped again in Karlstad Central. Two policemen boarded the train and came directly to where I was sitting.

"We have been informed that you are a Norwegian and we want to see your passport and your permit to travel in a frontier area."

(Foreigners were forbidden to enter Karlstad and its vicinity.)

Not having any papers, I was taken to Karlstad police station where, after waiting for an hour and a half, I was questioned by two police officers. The wait had been long enough for me to memorize an imaginary life history and a plausible reason for wanting to travel through Arvika. As I felt that I was probably still "wanted" by the Swedes, I did not dare give my true name; instead I called myself Gunnar Lier, and said that I was born on March 16, 1916 and was a law student. My father was Erik M. Lier, born 1885, employed at Erik

Rund's engineering works at Grefsen. My mother's name was Magda.

I had it all down pat, including a plausible account of who had got me accommodations and food in Stockholm and supplied me with money, especially the 8,500 Crowns in my suitcase. I also had an answer ready in case I was asked how I got to Stockholm in the first place. Luckily I had a Swedish railway timetable with me and was able to find out the correct train times. I decided to say that I had crossed from Röros to Femundsjöen and from there to Lofsdalen and so to Sveg. This, of course, was the route I had taken on that memorable journey, only in reverse. As I was going to say that I had done this just before Christmas, I must still remember when the various trains had left, so I looked these up and memorized them. As for the frontier guards, I knew from experience that it was not difficult to get past them.

The two Swedes treated the matter very seriously. It was understandable that they were not keen on having foreigners poking about Värmland, an industrial area that included the Bofors Works not far from Karlstad. I knew that several couriers who had been caught before me had either been expelled from Sweden or imprisoned for espionage, though not of course against Sweden.

The interrogation went well, but I realized the two Swedes wanted to check my statements about Stockholm. They asked if I could give them the names of any Norwegian refugees in Sweden, and whether it was the Norwegian or British Legation in Stockholm that had sent me. I denied that I had anything to do with either, being sure that it was best to keep the legations out of it. Instead, I said that the money had been subscribed by numbers of the refugees and was to be used for propaganda material to be distributed in Norway. I gave the names of Fehn and Morland (the two with whom I had crossed into Sweden) as my contacts in Stockholm and hoped they would be quick-witted enough to realize the difficult situation I had gotten myself into.

After the interrogation I was held in custody at the Karlstad police station.

I had felt that my first interrogation had gone all right, but the second was different. My interrogator on this occasion was the Police Chief himself. First, he asked if it was correct that I was a law student. When I replied that it was, he began to question me about my studies and he seemed regrettably familiar with the Norwegian curriculum. After a while he said:

"It seems remarkable, Mr. Lier, that you don't know the subject you have chosen to study. I can't see a Swedish law student answering the way you have."

He went on to express his doubts as to my being what I made myself out to be.

"But I am, sir," I assured him. "It's only that I haven't yet been able to get down to studying properly. It's wrong of me, perhaps. But there it is."

The interrogation continued. In the end the decent fellow seemed to accept my story, though I sensed that he was still of two minds about me.

The cell I was put in was comfortable and the food was excellent. So the days passed and became weeks, the weeks a month, and it was well into the second month before I learned that my case was to come before the magistrates on March 3. I now spent some of the time in the guardroom with the police. They were pretty decent to me, although still not altogether sure who and what I was.

I did not have to be in court when my case came up but I was warned that there was no telling what the outcome would be. At worst I would get two years' imprisonment. It was not the worst.

After a few days I was told that I had been acquitted on the espionage charge and was to be sent to a camp for Norwegian refugees at a place called Voxna, nearly 200 miles north of Stockholm. A policeman was my escort on the long train trip there. My 8500 Crowns had been confiscated, but otherwise the Swedes were pretty fair with me, considering the number of their laws I had broken.

Once at the camp, I got in touch with the Norwegian and British Legations in Stockholm and reported what had happened. There, too, I discovered what had become of my friends Morland and Fehn and how they had fared when the police came and questioned them about a certain law student of their acquaintance called Gunnar Lier. Fortunately, I had once used Gunnar Lier as a cover-name and the two had remembered this and caught on at once. They had "identified" me so promptly that the Swedes believed my story.

Being in that camp was interesting. Most of the refugees were young Norwegian boys of between fifteen and sixteen who had crossed the green frontier on their own initiative. The camp was well organized and a lot was done to keep the boys occupied. The great forests all around the place provided wonderful skiing. It was a real holiday, and

I soon recovered from the slackness induced by the long weeks of inactivity in my prison cell in Karlstad. But there was an overhanging sadness there. All these young lads had crossed the frontier hoping to reach England and join the Norwegian army; and here they were, stuck in Sweden.

After I had been in the camp two or three weeks, I was sent for by the Norwegian Legation in Stockholm. The people at the camp gave me an identity document for the journey, and I was told to report to the Shipping Department at the Legation. This I did, but first I went to my good friends at the British Legation. I found them cautious where I was concerned, but that was understandable in the circumstances. The Swedes, of course, would have welcomed an excuse to expel me.

At the Norwegian Legation I was told that I was to be sent to Gothenburg to help supplement the crew of a Norwegian boat lying there. This I realized must mean one of the ten "stay-put" boats, Norwegian ships that had been in Swedish ports when war broke out. The Germans were now putting pressure on the Swedes to have these interned or at least to prevent their being released. But the Swedes had raised their embargo on them, and they were now waiting for a chance to make a dash for England.

I was not particularly attracted by the idea of going to sea. I don't like the sea and I can't swim, and it seemed to me that those ex-embargo ships would be death traps. That opinion was pretty well justified for, of the ten that finally put out from Gothenburg in the spring of 1942, only two reached England. Six were sunk by the Germans and two were forced to turn back.

No, I didn't want to go to sea. I wanted to get back to Norway, if only because I had promised certain groups that I would come back with information and money. The Legation people were rather irritated when I told them I didn't want to be a sailor; but I insisted and as good as refused to go to Gothenburg. Instead, I made another approach to the British, this time through an intermediary, proposing that I go back to Norway to work for them. This proposal was accepted. I made out to the Swedes that I was going to Gothenburg, and fortunately they soon lost interest in the doings of Gunnar Lier.

There I was in Stockholm once more, again without papers, living here and there and doing my best to avoid the police.

My intermediary with the British, Daniel Ring, acted as a sort of liaison officer and was in touch with the various departments at the Norwegian Legation. It was he who gave me my assignments from the British. Our conference room was the kitchen of his flat and there from early morning until late at night we discussed what I was to do. In that kitchen I was introduced to others who had come from Norway, so I could obtain their contacts. Many more men than I used that kitchen and, when the question arose what code number I was to use from Oslo, I asked for 13. It was already taken. Ring himself was No. 12, and it was finally decided that I should be No. 24.

Among those members of the resistance movement I met in Ring's kitchen was one who had been leader of the famous coup at Ulleval Hospital outside Oslo, when a number of wounded men were snatched out of the Germans' clutches and spirited away. This man put me in touch with the head of 2 Group, Carl Armin Fürst. He and I were to have much to do with each other.

CHAPTER IV

Intelligence Agent in Oslo

As No. 24 I was thoroughly briefed by Daniel Ring and was soon ready to go. Ring's office came under the British SOE (Special Operations Executive) of which the Norwegian Independent Company No. 1 was then a part. The company had been in action in the Moloy raid, where it had lost its commander, Captain Linge. This was the company my friends and I would have joined, if we had reached England.

Now I was not to go back alone, but in company with the well-known athlete Otto Berg, who was also a policeman. Berg had a number of assignments in Norway and was going to put me in touch with several groups that were still active, despite a recent wave of arrests which had followed the milk strike.

This milk strike came after the German attack on Russia had given the occupied countries fresh hope, because the German army had perhaps bitten off more that it could chew. The Nazis had intensified their efforts against the Resistance movements. In autumn of 1941, Berlin ordered that hostages were to be shot as a deterrent. However, because this was done so often, people's feelings were numbed and it lost its effect. Early in September Heydrich himself came to Oslo. After this visit the terror really started in Norway. The shipyard workers at Akers struck over the smallness of the milk ration. Two of them, the leaders, were shot, twenty-five received heavy sentences, and one hundred and twenty-five were arrested.

Everything was well organized. We were given tickets to Arvika and on April 9, 1942, left Stockholm by the morning train. At Arvika we were to get in touch with a certain taxi driver. The excitement began after we had changed at Laxa into the Karlstad train. When we heard the ticket collector coming, I curled up in a corner and pretended to be asleep. I had given Berg my ticket, which he proffered with his own, but the precaution proved unnecessary, as it was a different man. There were police on the platform at Karlstad Central, but we sat still and no one bothered us.

We reached Arvika in the afternoon, but could go no further till darkness had fallen. We spent our waiting time in the local outfitter's cellar. The owner was very pro-Norwegian and ran considerable risks, then and later, to help us find the couriers who used that route. When it was dark, we changed into sports clothes and, leaving our Swedish suits in the cellar, sought out our taxi driver, who was most helpful and drove us southwest first to Tocksfors on the main road to the frontier; there he turned into a side road which led north, past three little lakes, for a dozen miles or so. Here he stopped and we got out. From there we were to continue on foot.

It was late evening and we met no one. We passed the last of the farms, which lay near the middle of the three lakes, and no one appeared to have seen or noticed us. About one o'clock we left the road where it turned west to continue into Norway, and went across country. We moved with the utmost caution, stopping every now and again to listen. The last thing we wanted was to walk into the arms of a Swedish patrol.

Then, at last, we were across and on Norwegian territory. We fished out our revolvers, which we had kept hidden at the bottom of our rucksacks as long as we were in Sweden, not wanting to have weapons visible on us if we were caught. All was quiet. We hurried down a lumbermen's road, really a slide for getting logs to the water. Down by this lake we had another contact. It was far into the night before we reached his farm, and there we got a few hours of sleep.

Just before dawn the farmer rowed us across the lake and we climbed up the road and walked along it to the next bus stop. We boarded the first bus going in the direction of Oslo, fifty miles away, and we reached it after an uneventful journey. Berg took me to a flat one floor up over a big bakery, into which we could look from the back windows. This was the flat of the owner of the bakery and the address was No. 30 Gronland Street. It was to become famous in the annals of the underground movement.

Berg, being well known in Oslo both as an athlete and policeman, had to stay indoors in the flat most of the time. I had the great advantage of not being "wanted," either by the Germans or by the Norwegian State Police, so I went to my old quarters at Therese Street, where I told the people in the flat that I had been on a long visit home. The State Police were a special department of the Norwegian police force, which had numbered two or three hundred before the war. After the occupation, the Germans got rid of all "untractable" elements and, by recruiting the worst elements of the small number of Norwegian Nazis, managed to nazify the force. The rest of the police were good patriots and many of them were active Resistance men.

Berg was only to stay in Oslo for a few days, but while there he put me in touch with numbers of people, including the head of Group 2. With all these I called myself Krogh. None of them knew my true name or where I lived.

I had to tear up my Norwegian identity card in that train in Sweden before I was arrested in Karlstad and, if I were to play the part of a law-abiding citizen, I needed a new identity card. I felt reasonably certain that, when the Swedish police were looking for me after Christmas, 1941, they had not informed the Norwegian police of the fact, so the most natural course seemed to be to apply for another card in Rjukan, where the first had been issued. So to Rjukan I went at the first opportunity, walked into the police station there, and told them I had lost my identity card and would they please issue me another. They made no difficulties about this, and I went off happily to pay a surprise visit to my parents. I told them that I had come back to Oslo to fight the Germans and, if they were ever asked what I was doing, they were to say that I had various auditing jobs in Oslo, where I was also trying to study economics.

Resistance work was nothing new to my parents. After the wave of terror following the milk strike at Akers in September, 1941, all wireless sets were confiscated and possession was a crime that got you sent to a concentration camp in Germany. At this time my mother was staying at the Therese Street flat and my room became a sort of reception center for sets people wanted to get rid of without surrendering them. These I then distributed among friends and acquaintances who were not afraid to use them in secret, even though they knew the penalty if they were discovered. I wanted to send three of the sets to Rjukan and I also had a rifle for the same destination. Mother offered to take them with her when she went home. So we put one of the sets in a big expanding suitcase, another in a case which also had the rifle lying on the bottom of it, and the third we made into a parcel. Mother sent these three pieces of luggage by carrier to the bus station. When she got them out, some Germans there seemed only too glad to take them across to the bus for her. It wasn't every day they were allowed to help such a charming Norwegian lady.

As I began renewing my contacts I discovered that several of them had been compromised and had had to escape to Sweden. The group of radio people for whom I had promised to obtain money and parts had been broken up by the Gestapo. But I soon got in touch with Knut Moyen who had gone on working away to build up Milorg, the Military Organization. I told him that I had come to Oslo to help and to keep in touch with the British in Stockholm. Moyen warned me that the Germans had learned a trick or two and were exercising considerably stricter control. It was becoming difficult to move about the city in safety.

My immediate concern was the assignments given me by the SOE office in Stockholm and through my various contacts—old and new—I was able to obtain most of the information required. This concerned the movement of German troops in Norway, quantity and quality of their equipment, the activities of the German fleet and air force, supplies, etc., and the results achieved by the British air raids. Another of my jobs was to arrange for the reception in various Norwegian towns of radio operators to be dropped by parachute with transmitters. So in Oslo, Kristiansand, Haugesund, Stavanger, Bergen, Alesund, Trondheim, and Lillehammer, I had to arrange quarters for these men—a place where they could live and operate their sets—and jobs from which they could absent themselves without attracting notice. These men were to be "legalized" in every way, to have proper ration cards, health cards, and the rest of it. Another easier task was to obtain telephone directories, guide books, timetables and copies of all Police proclamations, also bound volumes of the *Norwegian Police Gazette* and the official gazette in which all laws are published.

My first report, two full pages, was ready and coded. I was to send it with the two couriers who had come from Stockholm via Arvika. Our friend the Swedish outfitter there had helped them through the road blocks. We met at the flat of a young businessman called Hans Michelsen. Neither he nor his wife knew what fear was and were eager to do whatever they could. Michelsen gradually became the one I worked most closely with, and for the next two months it was mostly the people of 2 Group with whom I collaborated.

Two men in the Margarine Pool saw to the "export" of the couriers. The arrangement with Stockholm was that we should try to get in contact with each other roughly every ten days. When I left Stockholm, I had been slightly doubtful about what we were trying to do, but it all went far better than I dreamed it would. The first courier arrived from Stockholm on May 14. We met at a house in Ulleval Garden City, and on May 17 he left with my report.

This man and a second courier who soon had to be recruited to help him were athletes and came from the frontier district and so had contacts on the Swedish side. Thanks to these contacts they soon had organized a safe route across by Kongsvinger, and before long they were making the trip, including the train journey from Stockholm to Arvika (a good six and a half hours), in under twenty-four hours. They often bicycled to Oslo from the Swedish frontier, finding this the safest and most certain way.

In Oslo, the couriers often stayed at baker Andersen's flat at Gronland 30, an excellent place in those days when food was not easily come by in the city. The baker, his wife, and daughter did a tremendous lot for us and for many a hungry resistance worker. Apart from the food the advantage of the flat (and the real reason it was used so much) was the fact that the flat entrance was shared with the shop and bakery and there were always so many people going in and out that our comings and goings were not noticed.

My correspondence with Stockholm was conducted in code. None of the couriers knew the code. At first I had no one to help me with this correspondence and I had a horrible amount of paper work. The worst time of each week for me was when I had to sit down at my typewriter and write and code my reports. After a bit I got Michelsen to help me and things were much easier.

CHAPTER V

The Network Is Extended

The next and most important problem was finding a place to live where people did not know my name. I had to get in touch with a new set of people and create an entirely new identity for myself. In this new milieu people must not know that I was doing underground work, or at least not to any extent that would make me interesting. And so, gradually, I acquired a circle of acquaintances and collaborators who had no idea who I really was.

I held one trump card—I did not look as though I could be engaged in any serious resistance work. I was of medium height, of fairly ordinary appearance and looked good-natured and easy-going. I had no distinguishing marks in the passport sense and my dress was as ordinary and unobtrusive as I could make it, usually a suit of grey gabardine and neutral shirts and ties. The only possible perplexity to people who knew me well was the fact that I was perhaps slightly shabby compared to what I had been while I had my auditor's job.

There were plenty of families in and around Oslo who had hidden resistance workers, but to have one living permanently with one was a very different business.

I had a succession of rooms in various parts of the city and suburbs, taking with me the essentials of my wardrobe from Therese Street. In order not to be seen too much in the neighborhood where I was living, I went out in the morning and did not return until the evening. I was always armed and slept with my pistol under my pillow, because the Germans liked to make their captures between four and five in the morning. I tried to keep my pistol hidden, so as not to cause my hosts unnecessary anxiety, but one morning I forgot it and left it under my pillow. My landlady at the time was an undauntable woman who had no scruples about hiding any number of Resistance men, and when I went back to retrieve my pistol she was already doing my room and I found her standing there with the pistol in her hand. All she said was:

"I've one like this too."

Gradually I acquired a number of homes where I could have lunch and other meals. I kept away from restaurants and, if there was any place I visited regularly, it was baker Andersen's flat at Gronland 30. This may have been because of a great weakness for cakes and pastries, and this was the only place in wartime Oslo where I could indulge it. Little by little I cached toilet things and a basic wardrobe at each of my hideouts. I used a number of cover-names, usually Krogh, and took great care to see that as few as possible knew my various "places." At first, it was quite a job remembering who knew which place and even which name; later I did it quite automatically.

Shortly after my return I went to see friends among the police at Notodden, a town eighty miles to the southwest of Oslo. Almost the entire police force was now in the resistance movement and one of them at Notodden, Sverre Svendsen, had suggested that he try to get into the State Police in Oslo. We realized that to have a reliable informant there would be of inestimable value. Svendsen's idea was accepted and he began circumspectly to make himself appear a reliable and suitable candidate for the Nazis' police force.

A problem that soon confronted me was that of supplies. It was not that I personally had difficulties over ration cards; baker Andersen and others of my contacts saw to that; but as time went on others had to be helped and I had to take food to my various hideouts. I received a lot of welcome aid from the supply organization of 2 Group, which had depots of food and plenty of ration cards, but I felt that I needed to be independent of 2 Group. In the end I found a splendid source in another of the Esso people with whom I had begun to work. This man, Thorp, had to travel in the countryside around Oslo and had numbers of good contacts. One was a big wholesaler in Drammen who was a splendid source of groceries. Baker Andersen had put me in touch with a woman in the sales organization of the Norwegian dairies and she seemed to have an inexhaustible supply of cheese, butter, and eggs. I also knew a warehouseman in the same organization, and he was a great help to me and many others all through the war.

Through Knut Moyen I was still in contact with Milorg. Moyen was very cautious, and few people had direct access to him. I often wondered that he was prepared to meet me, but of course he knew that the Germans were not on the lookout for me and that I lived the whole time under cover. Moyen's caution proved of inestimable value after I left Norway in October, 1941, for the Germans were then successful in breaking up the whole Military Organization, especially in Oslo, arresting several of its officers, and forcing others to escape to Sweden. Contact with the country districts was cut and Moyen, one of the few who were uncompromised and able to do the job, had a difficult time building it all up again. He had a number of good helpers, including a young lad of eighteen or nineteen, Erling Lorentzen, a member of a well-known shipping family, who, years later, was to marry Princess Ragnhild.

Being a good organizer, Moyen had arranged for a successor in case anything should happen to him or he should have to flee the country. His choice was a man called Jens Chr. Hauge who had become known as a great opponent of the Nazis through the lectures he had given to students in 1940-41. Moyen had had to persuade him to keep his mouth shut, at least on this subject, and he had since dropped out of the public eye and was pretty well forgotten. There was no need for me to know Moyen's successor-elect and I wasn't told, but I learned about it by other ways. Hauge later became Norwegian Defense Minister at the age of thirty and was Minister of Justice from 1954 to 1955.

At the end of April, 1942, there was a tragic occurrence in the west. Two men had been brought from England and landed at Televag on the island of Sotra off Bergen. Someone gave the show away and the Germans appeared on the scene. There was a violent exchange of gunfire and one of the men was shot. A few days later the Germans came back and razed the place to the ground. Three hundred houses and farm buildings were burned, cattle were slaughtered, and all boats destroyed. The eighty adult males were deported to Germany, where most of them died before the war ended. Two hundred and sixty women and children were expelled and interned in Norway.

This ghastly business made Moyen take up the whole question of agents from Britain. Moyen thought it most unfortunate that SOE had organized all this independently and asked me to pass on his views. A few days later his case was further strengthened when two more SOE men were arrested, one in Drammen and one in Moss (on either side of Oslo fjord, south of the city), and their arrest involved several of the Milorg people, including Moyen, who just managed to extricate himself. I saw Moyen that evening and heard how the Germans had been within an ace of getting their hands on him. What had happened was this: Moyen had sent Erling Lorentzen to Drammen to find out the position with the Milorg organization there. Lorentzen discovered that several of the leaders had been arrested and went straight back to Oslo to report. A few days later Lorentzen came to Moyen with a bicycle they were to have a look at and send away to a place in the country. Moyen and Lorentzen went down to the courtyard of the building, leaving Moyen's wife alone in the flat. The telephone rang and when Mrs. Moyen answered it, a voice said he was Engineer Lund, that he knew her husband and would very much like to come up and see him. When Moyen and Lorentzen went up to the flat and were told of the telephone conversation, Moyen wondered, because there was no Engineer Lund among his contacts or connections. When his wife added that the man had spoken with a slight accent, he knew what was afoot. Soon there was a ring at the front door, and Moyen and Lorentzen disappeared down the back stairs; as they went down, they heard Mrs. Moyen opening the door to Engineer Lund, who happened to be Gestapo-man Fehmer. He walked straight in and asked for Moyen. Mrs. Moyen said that he was in the courtyard, but would be coming up any moment. The Gestapo man sat down to wait. Meanwhile Moyen and Lorentzen had reached the ground floor. Peeping out, they saw several Gestapo men in the street. There was only one thing to do: Taking the bicycle between them, they coolly walked towards the Germans, almost strolling along, whistling a popular tune and laughing and joking. The Germans looked at them attentively as they passed, but did nothing more. As soon as they were around the corner, the two put on a spurt.

They remained in hiding in Oslo for two or three weeks; then we managed to get them to our man in Kongsvinger who saw them safely across the frontier.

The cause of these disasters was faulty organization in England and lack of liaison. Televag was being used by two organizations independently of each other. SOE had used it on several occasions to land men from the Norwegian Independent Company, while the Norwegian section of SIS had also sent ships to land their secret agents there. All those boats coming from England made people talk, especially as the crew of one of the ships had shown themselves on deck in naval uniform. This inevitably led to tragedy.

In this period I usually used a bicycle for getting about Oslo. It was the safest and most certain means of communication and, if you ran into a control post in a street, it gave you a chance to get away. But I began to need a car more and more. Through 2 Group I got in touch with a man who owned and drove a taxi, A-5032, and from then on he did a lot of driving for me. He took the couriers on the first stage of their journey east, saving over forty miles' pedalling and a good many hours' time. I used the man when I had packets or parcels to deliver. Once we drove all the way to Halden when I had to rush a message to Stockholm in order to stop a wrong report. The quickest way was via Halden and Bokerod, so to Halden we went, eighty-three miles away. We reached it in two hours and a half. An hour later a man was on his way to the frontier with the message, which reached Stockholm in time. Unfortunately, my taxi driver was arrested a few days afterwards in connection with a "dispatch" of refugees and the poor man spent several years in Grini prison. I got myself another taxi with another driver.

One of my main tasks in Oslo was to set up a proper center, a place to collect all our information and where the Stockholm office's couriers could attend to letters and reports. This meant a safe location so a visit there would involve the least possible danger. Another and equally important job was to expand my network of contacts and information sources.

Much of my work required my being in Oslo, the rest necessitated travel, so there was a certain conflict there. My instructions were that, if I had information of particular urgency, I was to try to send it directly to England. I had two methods available. Group 2 had a transmitter and was in contact with England, and I also had contact with one of Milorg's transmitters and could use that in an emergency.

The couriers from Stockholm were so familiar with the drill now that they arrived on the dot every time. I would have my reports ready and they would give me my new instructions. Stockholm was able to give me a lot of help. Many people passed through Daniel Ring's office in Sweden; from them he took useful names and information. Thus, when I was given a new task, I was often also given the names of those who might help.

One of these couriers was Erik Reichelt, who later was lost while with the *Brattholm*, one of the Shetland boats which took part in the famous North Norway Expedition.

The expedition—the longest trip made by any of the Shetland boats —was to land men in northern Norway to organize sabotage groups, set up Milorg groups, give instruction in the use of arms, and maintain radio contact with Great Britain. Unfortunately, one storekeeper they contacted was a traitor, and he informed the German Security Police in Tromso. There was a fight in which two of the men were wounded— one of them later dying of his wounds—and eight were taken to Tromso. They were tortured for thirty-six hours, then taken outside the town and shot. There was only one survivor.

All this time we used the Kongsvinger route. Our key man on this route was in Kongsvinger. He was called Hans Engebretsen and he and his family lived in a house, where he also had his offices, on the Oslo road just as you enter the town. Up to 1941 he had run a local newspaper, but when this had to stop in September, 1941, he switched to transport and haulage and was in an excellent position to obtain all sorts of information. He was as cautious as he was daring. No outsider ever learned what he did for us. He didn't even let his family know.

From Kongsvinger, the couriers bicycled out on the middle of the three roads to the frontier as far as Austmarka, beyond which there was a Customs house on the Swedish side. There we had another man who owned a farm on the frontier. The farmer and his wife were an elderly couple, but they had two sons. One, a young man of twenty-five, acting on instructions from the Resistance Movement, pretended to be a Nazi and even joined the NS party, so as to safeguard the couriers' route. He played his part so well that he acquired a nasty reputation among his patriotic countrymen, but that farm was the main crossing place on the Stockholm route up to the end of the war. The whole family were heart and soul in the resistance movement. The three men were wonderful woodsmen and knew every inch of the ground even far over on the Swedish side. Time and again they guided couriers across to the various Swedish hamlets. Every now and again the farm received a visit from the Germans and when there was a courier there, as happened on several occasions, the man had to stay upstairs quiet as a mouse, a nerve-racking business. But there was never any trouble.

The courier would wait till the darkest part of the night and then walk through the forest and rejoin the road on the Swedish side, where we had bicycles hidden. From there he would ride to Arvika and catch a train.

Through 2 Group I met a young student who put me in touch with Naval Intelligence. I had contact with the clandestine newspaper people. Gradually I was expanding my network of agents, as well as my own hideouts. I was always using new cover names and none of my landlords knew where I spent my days or where I ate. Thus there was no risk of them knowing too much, if they should be arrested.

Our agents in the police convinced us that we could not count on people being able to keep their mouths shut when interrogated by German methods. Many people were fantastically brave and some even endured a Gestapo interrogation without being broken, but these were the exceptions that proved the general rule. We felt it improper and unfair to assume that those who were arrested would be able to give nothing away, and we acted accordingly.

The Televag business had had a tremendous effect on morale. It was understandable after the Germans' atrocities there that people tended to avoid close contact with resistance workers. Of course, no one ever refused to help and there were those who volunteered to give shelter to people who had to go into hiding. These people ran terrible risks. Anything might happen if the Germans caught them sheltering a wanted person, including death. But to us, places to stay and places to hide were a matter of life and death, the foundation of all resistance work. The Germans' interrogation methods were brutal and those who were sent to Germany regarded it as a relief. It meant the end of interrogation and a better chance of survival—or so it was thought. None of us—the prisoners least of all—yet knew the significance of the stamp NN (Nacht and Nebel) that appeared on the papers of many who were thus deported, destined for an extermination camp.

Baker Andersen knew two men in the prison service, who could tell us what happened to those who were arrested. On occasion I was even able to go and see the prisoners. To achieve this, the person concerned had to pretend to be ill. Sometimes we were able to smuggle drugs to them that would produce symptoms, to fool the German doctor and get them sent to hospital. That was the way in which a number managed to escape during 1941 and 1942. Altogether I made several visits to Ulleval Hospital to talk with prisoners who had information.

Hans Michelsen continued his work for me, and his home soon became a headquarters for couriers to and from Stockholm. He decoded reports and coded the ones that we were sending. His business allowed him to travel about the West country and he made many such trips solely on our account, arranging accommodations for radio telegraphers and the like. He ran considerable risks, all the more so as he continued to live in his own flat and would have been easy to capture.

Much as Michelsen did for me, I needed more help, and it struck me that perhaps it would be best to bring back someone who had left Norway early enough to be forgotten now. That idea made me think of Per Morland, my friend from the Students' Hut whom I had left in Uppsala when I came back to Norway in April, 1942. As far as I knew, he was still there. He had not been happy with his lot, for he hated studying in Uppsala instead of joining the Norwegian Forces in England. I sent word to Stockholm that I would like to have Morland sent back, and one day at the end of May he arrived with the courier.

Morland came from Horten, a town well down Oslo Fjord. Those who knew him in Oslo were almost entirely students, and few of them knew he had gone to Sweden in 1941. At first, he was very careful, but that was only while he familiarized himself with the situation. After a few weeks he had given up making detours and was riding straight through the center of the city. He was our "missing link," and those he linked never knew each other's addresses or meeting places. He continued this work in Oslo right up to the liberation, except for a few holidays in Sweden. The Gestapo had been interested in him in 1941, which was why he had gone to Sweden, but later they never discovered what he was doing.

Morland quickly made himself independent of my contacts, finding his own, who remained unknown to me. That made things more difficult in certain ways, since we had to have separate hideouts and avoid being seen much together: but the two of us working in that way accomplished a great deal more than if we had worked strictly together. It was our report of June 16-17 that alerted London that the *Tirpitz* was about to sail from Trondheim and appeared to be intact.

Milorg had many difficulties in those days and no great confidence in London. We were made to feel this too, especially when we got orders to have as little to do with Milorg as possible—a very difficult order to obey fully—and I had to retain some cautious contacts. London could not realize what Milorg was going to develop into and I had to adopt a wait-and-see policy. Later I heard that even London was beginning to realize that there was no point in sending arms instructors back to Norway unless there was proper liaison with Milorg.

My policeman friend at Notodden, Sverre Svendsen, had been playing his part so well that he could now get into the Nazis' State Police. I reported this to the leader of the political group I was in contact with, and he agreed that Svendsen ought to take the job. And he did. He moved to Oslo, got himself a flat, and began to work for the State Police.

CHAPTER VI

All Sorts of Things Happen

In order to keep the Kongsvinger-Austmarka route safe for the Stockholm couriers, it was decided to close it to refugees, whoever they might be. This decision made it necessary to find another route so refugees could get out of the country. For this we did not have to go very far. Sixteen miles to the south of Austmarka is Magnor, where the main Oslo-Stockholm railway line crosses the frontier. This is a densely wooded forest district and was eminently suitable for the purpose. The route we planned involved turning off the main Oslo-Kongsvinger road at Skarnes, forty miles from Oslo; from there taking a secondary road to Disena, then on foot through the forest to Vestmarka, south of Magnor, where there was a customs station, and so to the frontier. There was a lake on the frontier which made a convenient crossing place. The lake was on a farm of one of the forest wardens, a man called Sommerfeldt. This man had already helped people across, and one of our couriers had even used the route on a couple of occasions. We now wished to get it properly organized for the refugee traffic, so one day I paid a visit to a man who was one of the directors of the big lumber company that owned and exploited the forests round Disena and Vestmarka. What I wanted was to have one of our men on the spot, and this meant getting him a sham job with the company—preferably as a forester—and having him work near the border. It was soon arranged. We now had three exporters: the antique dealer I have already mentioned, No. 2 Group, and a man who had a men's outfitters' shop near Majorstue. His shop acted as a post office and exchange for refugee information. The traffic was well organized.

One of our resistance men was a policeman called Ropstad, who drove a car in the so-called Schnell-kommando, an emergency patrol mainly concerned with traffic control. He was a daring fellow and did a lot for us. On one occasion, one of the Stockholm couriers had to get to a number of places in Oslo. Ropstad drove him around in the kommando car. On several occasions the courier found himself sharing it with Germans, but all went well. Then things went wrong—or very nearly. Ropstad helped a man get a travel permit to go to Trondheim. The man was arrested and unfortunately let out Ropstad's name, and he was arrested. The charge was a trivial one and the situation would not have been dangerous except that Ropstad had on him a list of names and cover names. The list included my name—at least my cover name—and that of the man who ran the supply organization for 2 Group. Ropstad would have had a difficult time explaining how he came to know him. Ropstad managed to send a warning to this man, Karlson, but the message did not reach him and he was arrested. The situation became ominous. Karlson was carrying a suitcase full of stamps used for faking passports when he was arrested, and that made his arrest a serious matter for Ropstad.

Between them, these two men knew a great deal about our underground work, and the situation was grave for a number of people. In fact it was so serious that our men in the police began discussing the possibility of getting Ropstad and Karlson out. This was where Sverre Svendsen, by then well established in the Nazi State Police, came into his own. His plan was that he should issue written orders for the two men to be fetched from prison for interrogation at State Police Headquarters. They could then disappear on the way. This would mean the end of Svendsen's career in the State Police, but he was prepared to accept that. Anyway he suspected that his superiors had not been as enthusiastic about his work lately as before, so the time might be ripe for him to get out in any case. After a little discussion, it was decided to sacrifice Svendsen for the sake of getting out the two men who knew so much that could be dangerous to so many.

Svendsen was an unusually cool customer, but this was not a job that he could do alone. He had to have an assistant—someone to drive the car he was to fetch the prisoners in. The action was planned by another policeman familiar with conditions at the prison.

It was morning when a car drove up to the prison in Akebergveien. In the back seat were the State Police with papers requiring two prisoners, Ropstad and Karlson, to be handed over for further interrogation at State Police Headquarters. Everything went like clockwork. The Germans handed the two prisoners over without a murmur and the car drove away. Ropstad and Karlson were free, but Svendsen was hopelessly compromised and had to go into hiding. We hid him in a flat for several days, till we judged the worst of the excitement had subsided, and then sent him out of the country via the Halden "export" route, which seemed the safest. This meant his leaving Oslo by train from the East Station. As he was "wanted," the risk was considerable, so we decided that he must be disguised. We were thorough and dyed his hair. It was the first time I had seen it done and I was very interested in the technique. The actual job was done by a woman hairdresser. When she had finished with him, Svendsen looked most extraordinary. His hair was a peculiar shade of red so obviously unnatural that it could not have failed to arouse suspicion. The woman had another try and managed to make him look more or less plausible. So, with his new haircoloring, Svendsen rode to the station, bought his ticket, and reached the rendezvous in Halden without further adventure. There our people took him across the frontier into safety. Ropstad and Karlson also got across, but by a different route.

After Ropstad's escape, baker Anderson felt he must be careful, as it was reasonable to assume that the State Police knew that Ropstad had been a frequent visitor to Gronland Street 30. To be on the safe side, Andersen went to his hut in the mountains near Vinje for a while, where I saw him once or twice. While I was there in the second half of July, the police paid their anticipated visit to Gronland Street. Learning that Andersen was at his hut in the mountains, the police got onto three of the local deputy sheriffs and ordered them to investigate and report if there was anything suspicious about the hut and Andersen's presence there. The three were cautioned to be circumspect and to make sure that they were always armed.

We spent a few enjoyable days at the hut, where all was very peaceful until one evening, as we sat chatting, I suddenly became prey to a strange restlessness and something inside urged me to go to Rjukan, which was some thirty-five miles northeast of us. I think this was the first time this strange restlessness came over me. Later, it was to prove an infallible warning of approaching or impending danger. I cannot explain it, but suppose that it was a form of intuition, a sort of extra sense developed to supply the needs of one who lived the life I did. Anyway, on this occasion I followed the promptings of my instinct and left the baker's hut at midnight, walked down to the hamlet, picked up my bicycle, and rode to Rjukan.

I had not long left the hut before visitors began to arrive. The first were two Resistance men, Morland and Holth-Larsen, the latter having just come from Stockholm with an important message for me. Then three deputy sheriffs arrived, equally unexpectedly, but not till between four and five in the morning. They had a whole army with them and looked pretty foolish when they found some thoroughly ordinary people on a perfectly normal mountain holiday. They did, however, arrest Andersen and his daughter, Reidun, who was there with him. The two were taken to prison, but they had a plausible explanation of their presence at the hut and, as the State Police were unable to find any connection with resistance work, they were released after six days.

Although he was free, we were a bit hesitant to make use of baker Andersen and his flat. It was probable that the State Police or the Germans would pay further visits to 30 Gronland Street, and the consequences could be disastrous if we were caught there. But time passed and nothing happened, and gradually we began visiting Andersen's flat as before.

Stockholm gave me more and more varied assignments. There was a wireless transmitter that had to be taken to an operator in Vestlandet. A courier brought the set from Stockholm. When he got to Kongsvinger, he fastened it onto the carrier of his bicycle, swung himself into the saddle and rode off with it—all 450 miles to Vestlandet.

Then in the autumn, we were told to take charge of another wireless operator coming from England and see that he got properly established. He arrived with the Stockholm courier, who took him to a house in Ulleval Garden Suburb. He turned out to be a chap I had met in Stockholm, from where he had been sent to England for training. We had to put him in touch with the head of Milorg's communication group. From the security point of view, it was perhaps not ideal that we should know where the man was living and were mixed up with Milorg's communication, but there was no other way of helping him. We installed him in a flat and later he acted as our link with England, when we had urgent information to send.

We also had to collect funds to finance our work. This was the job of a man in the newspaper *Morgenbladet,* Jens Lodrup. He was getting on in years but he worked night and day for us, until the Germans nearly got him and he had to get across to Sweden in a hurry, from where he went to London.

We had a number of shops which we used as post offices and meeting places. At one, a sports shop, Morland and I met almost every day right up to the end of the war. There was a furrier's, too, and we used the suit department at the big store, Steen and Strom. When you had no permanent address or residence, it wasn't always easy to get the coupons you needed to buy anything made of cloth, so our Steen and Strom contact was invaluable.

Another contact of tremendous help was Mrs. Collett, the owner of a fashionable furniture shop. She was in touch with the wife of Admiral Hammerich in Copenhagen and the two of them had for some time worked a little scheme so that a good proportion of the food parcels from Denmark benefited the people in prison. As time went on she was able to divert part of the supplies to various underground organizations. She had a store of Danish food in the cellars under her shop, and many were the visits I made to it.

The Germans were now being more thorough and energetic in their investigations, and a number of my contacts had dropped out of the picture. The agent with the men's outfitters up at Majorstue was arrested in May, and later sent to Germany where he died in a concentration camp. Of course, the Germans' control posts in the street were pretty innocuous. There was little a German could find out from an identity card however false it might be, and unless you were carrying something very suspicious on you, you were fairly certain of getting through.

Morland and I kept a wary eye on everything that went on. We were always in good spirits, and, some people thought, too inclined to play the fools. Perhaps we were sometimes reckless, but often we had to be —especially when there might be compromising things in the rooms of someone the Germans had just arrested, things that had to be rescued. Then we would pose as self-appointed "Controllers," break the seals the Germans had put on the door, and go in and remove what dangers we could find. This was a game that could easily have gone wrong, but we developed a wonderful "nose" and never got into difficulties.

When the Germans tried to get Moyen and he escaped, they arrested his wife and took her away. In Moyen's flat were 20,000 Crowns of Milorg funds that he was hiding. This had to be rescued—a little job that fell to Morland, me, and another man. While in the flat, we purloined some of Mrs. Moyen's homemade jam. In doing so we were smeared with some strange green stuff, which we imagined had been sprinkled on the shelves to betray any thieves.

I got some of it in my hair and we had a lot of fun. We never discovered what it was. But that was not the end of the story. Some time later the third man's sister was arrested and we sent some of the jam to her in prison. She happened to be in the same cell as Mrs. Moyen, who was astonished to see her own jam being eaten in notorious Grini Prison.

CHAPTER VII

The Bank of Norway Coup

In the autumn of 1942 Stockholm gave us an intriguing job. London wanted printing plates for the 5-, 10-, 50-, and 100-Crown notes from the Bank of Norway's printers. The necessary names were sent me by the omniscient Daniel Ring in Stockholm and soon we were seeing a man who had a friend who was managing director of the Bank of Norway's printers.

London did not need the originals—casts would do. I was also asked to obtain a large specimen of the paper on which the notes were printed. The printer took the matter up with the head of the bank. It was a risky business and would have serious consequences if anything went wrong. Could they hand these valuable objects over to a young man of twenty-three or -four whom they had never seen before and whose real name they did not even know? To steal the plates would be exceedingly difficult, for a strict account was kept of them, and having matrices made would have aroused suspicions. If the Germans smelled a rat it would mean the death sentence.

For security reasons, I did not go to see the Bank's printers myself, but left this part of the business to our contact man. This was towards the end of August, 1942. Then one day he came to see me and told me that the printers insisted on proof that responsible authorities in London were behind the plan.

"What proof do they want?" I asked.

"A letter from Toralv Oksnevad" (a radio announcer, known to everyone in Norway as "the voice from London."

"And what is to be in the letter?"

He wrote down what the letter was to contain. I reported this to Stockholm, which passed the information to London. A short time later I received a letter for the printers from Oksnevad.

To borrow the plates it was necessary to put the Bank of Norway in the picture. Obviously, if the stamps were taken while they were in transit, a number of persons would get into difficulties, so a hold-up was not practicable.

The final arrangement was that the plates were to be handed to me one afternoon and I would try to get them across the frontier and into Sweden that same night. Meanwhile, those implicated would go into hiding until I gave the word that all was well again.

The moment I received the little parcel of plates, I went to my taxi driver, put the parcel at the bottom of a sack of charcoal (used in his gas-generator), and at eight o'clock we set out for Kongsvinger. At first all went well, but when we were on the straight stretch of road the other side of Klofta, twenty miles from Oslo, the car's lights suddenly went out. It was pitch dark, the car skidded and ended in the ditch. There we were, not very pleased with ourselves. To obtain help and get the car out of the ditch would not be easy at that place and time, apart from the fact that we weren't eager to have outsiders wondering about us.

Before long, a giant six-wheeled German truck came along. We stopped it and asked for help. The Germans were delighted at being asked to help Norwegians, as they—the ordinary soldiers at least—usually were, and together we had the car back on the road, fortunately undamaged, within a quarter of an hour. We then drove on to Engebretsen's office at Kongsvinger and he arranged for the parcel's transport across the frontier, while we drove back to Oslo. At eight o'clock the next morning I was able to ring our contact and tell him that all was well and that those involved could come out of hiding.

In Stockholm the parcel was delivered to Daniel Ring, who had got hold of a friendly blockmaker, and instructed him in what to do. In the utmost secrecy, he made two sets of matrices, and that same day the original plates were on their way back to Oslo by courier and the next day back in their proper place.

One set of matrices was sent to England via SOE with the British plane, and the second set followed the next day with the Norwegian plane.

So far my work had gone well. I had gotten myself established in Oslo without the Germans having any interest in me. One man who had been arrested had given away the name of Krogh, but he could tell them nothing except that he believed I was engaged in the transport of refugees to Sweden. I now had excellent connections in a number of spheres, half of whom had no knowledge of what I was called or where I came from. Most believed I was Oslo-born.

Late in the autumn of 1942 I went to Stockholm to report and be briefed for further work. It was easier to stay in Stockholm now. The couriers had got flats for themselves and I was able to stay with them without registering or reporting to the police.

During this short stay in Stockholm I became better acquainted with Consul Tom Nielsen, SOE's Stockholm chief, and his assistant at that time, Mrs. Waring. Mrs. Waring was the wife of a British diplomat in Stockholm and had rendered us sterling service ever since April, 1940. The Swedes, however, came to the conclusion that she had gone far beyond the limit of what they could turn a blind eye to. This was partly because in April, 1940, Mrs. Waring with SOE's former chief, Malcolm Munthe, son of the famous Axel Munthe, had tried to rescue Norwegians from prison in Stockholm. Their plan had not come off, and Munthe was turned out of the country.

Nielsen had lived a long time in Norway. To look at him, you would have said that he was the most peaceable man alive and it was difficult to conceive that he was behind all these "shady" doings in Stockholm. These four days or so in Stockholm were a wonderful holiday as far as I was concerned. It was lovely being able to roam about well-lit streets, look into shop windows, and eat what you wanted to eat. The contrast with Oslo was tremendous. The spring of 1942 had been very bad in Norway as far as food was concerned.

Ring now told me that soon I would have to help agents that would be sent into Norway via Stockholm, which meant that the Swedes were more inclined to shut their eyes to certain things where our struggle in Norway was concerned. We discussed the difficulties these agents from England had with Milorg and the need for closer cooperation between England and the military organization in Norway. I explained how I had tried to keep apart from Milorg, only to find that I was compelled by circumstances to remain in touch and do what I could to support it, and consequently still had good contacts there.

Before going back to Norway, which I did via the couriers' Arvika-Kongsvinger route, I went to see the Norwegian Military Office and its branch where all Norwegian refugees coming to Sweden were interrogated, to learn if certain people still in Norway were compromised or implicated, so I might warn them in time.

Our new forest route was now in use. We had got hold of a man called Aubert to be our frontier guide. He was an excellent skier with a good sense of direction and was willing to work as a lumberman. He had been taken on by the lumber company and sent up to the forests between Skarnes and Vestmarka, where he lived all by himself, so that the long trips he had to make to familiarize himself with the terrain did not attract attention.

One of the first people to use the route was baker Andersen. That autumn was a bad time for the Military Organization and a number of them had to get out, especially after the fateful state of emergency in Trondelag in October. Altogether quite a number of important people used our new route. It was for their kind that we had planned it and meant to reserve it. But when one of the men in Shell asked us to help a whole family out of the country into Sweden, where the husband and father already was, we concluded that our new forest route would be too much for women and children and that we would have to arrange something quite different. The final arrangement was that they were to go by train to Kongsvinger and even beyond, to one of the stations just before Magnor, and from there Aubert would guide them across the frontier, a fairly simple undertaking. That, however, was not how things worked out.

By some unfortunate coincidence the family was recognized at Kongsvinger and Aubert only just managed to get away. He reported the failure of the plan to us, and warned another man whom he was taking and who was in the station restaurant at the time. The man managed to slip out of the restaurant and got away, but the news reached us too late to warn the man in Shell. The Germans got there first. The Shell man's contact with us, a director of the lumber company, was of course implicated. We managed to get word to him and he fled from home, but unfortunately he had some dangerous papers at his office and, when he went there for them, the Germans were sitting there waiting and he was arrested.

After this, Aubert could not continue with the route and it was not used again. Aubert himself went to Stockholm and eventually became one of our couriers.

A great friend—and school friend—of mine, Halvor Rivrud, now joined me to act as my deputy or shadow and take over my work with Morland if I was captured. Rivrud's reputation was spotless as far as the Germans were concerned and, apart from Morland and me, no one knew that he had joined us. Since he was so thoroughly "safe," we felt it would be all right for him and a mutual school friend from Rjukan to live in my old room in Therese Street. This other friend had just finished reading law and was thinking of going in for Resistance work, of which he already had gotten a taste.

One of my close collaborators at this time put me in touch with a man who owned a filling station near the Guards Barracks in Slemdalsveiden (one of the main roads out of the city). He had a flat there which became one of our meeting places. I had acquired various hiding places and secret stores where all our material and equipment were hidden away. These stores ranged from whole cellars to broom-cupboards in buildings, where the caretaker was one of us.

The complex of places in which we slept, ate, worked, met, and stored our things was incredibly complicated—it had to be—and only Morland and I knew all its ramifications. It would have been an advantage if we two could have kept our various compartments watertight, but that was impossible. If I were caught or compromised, Morland would have to take over at once and therefore it was essential for him to know everything. We kept firearms wherever we slept and always locked our doors at night; for we did not intend to be taken without a fight. To keep our shooting skills, we went out into the country regularly for target practice.

CHAPTER VIII

Things Get More Difficult

In the last days of October, 1942, two good contacts of mine were caught. One was engaged in the export of refugees. On October 27 he had brought a group to Halden and was taking them up to the frontier near there, when they were seen by a frontier guard. The man shot the guard, but unfortunately did not manage to get away. He was arrested and later shot. The game was getting more difficult and hazardous, and we had to be more careful than ever.

Morland's was a name, I felt, that would never get out. He had used a cover name from the very first in Oslo. With me it was different. Perhaps there were too many who knew me, including agents who had come from England. None of us suspected that the Germans would make such a drive for me as they did, when they finally established my identity.

The courier service was working like a well-oiled machine, and on December 18 I wrote my twenty-third report. We also had the satisfaction of knowing that our organization had carried on after others had broken down. After the state of emergency in Trondheim in October, the messages from Trondheim had to be sent down to us in Oslo and we sent them on to Stockholm over our route. Conditions in Trondheim were pretty hopeless then, but luckily our contact, a railwayman, was never discovered. His opposite number at the East station in Oslo was the stationmaster himself.

We manufactured our own passports and permits of various kinds. I had learned the art when I was working closely with No. 2 Group. We had two contacts at the newspaper *Morgenposten* who got us any sort of printing plate we wanted made. All we had to provide was a sample impression and the paper. Our contacts were so good that, when the Nazis decided to make various tiny incisions in the forms used for identity cards and permits, we heard of it at once and were able to see that our plates had exactly the same "authentic" cuts in them.

At the end of September I had learned via Rjukan that the production of heavy water was about 130 litres a month, of which 100 were sent to Germany. At this time I was in touch with Einar Skinnarland. Skinnarland had been in England on Easter 1942, and had come back; he was also one of those who, with Odd Starheim, had captured the coastal passenger ship *Galtesund* and sailed her to England.

In the middle of June, Stockholm asked me to tell Skinnarland that he was to stay in Norway and be prepared to receive a man from England who was going to be dropped by parachute near Mosvann, Skinnarland's home town, some time after August 22. Skinnarland was to listen to the British Broadcasting Corporation for a special code message which would tell him the date. On July 14 Stockholm asked me to tell Skinnarland that the man was coming at the end of August, and instructed me to help him in any way I could. Just before this I had been asked to get hold of a bottle of heavy water from the plant at Vemork outside Rjukan. That had not been a simple matter, but we had managed it and the bottle had reached London safely. On September 30 I received instructions to get word as quickly as possible to Einar Skinnarland that he was to be sent certain equipment from England, which would be dropped by parachute at the spot near Lake Mosvann they had already used successfully. Skinnarland was to listen to the news from London and if the announcer said "*Dette er siste nyhetene fra London*" it would mean that the plane was coming that same night.

At the end of August, Stockholm asked us if we could get particulars of the various "protected areas" off the Norwegian coast. We took this to mean that the boats from Shetland were not having an easy time of it and that it was the famous Shetland Larsen and his gang who needed the information.

Were these areas mined? How many mines had been laid? What did the German patrol boats look like? What armament did they carry? What sort of passes and permits did fishing boats require for these forbidden zones?

Apparently one of the boats from Shetland had tried to get to Silda after the new restrictions had been imposed by the Germans. It had gone to the seaward of Vagsoy but, just after it had entered the zone, it had encountered a large fishing boat that the Germans had armed and were using as a patrol boat. The Shetland boat had turned at once and got away.

The Lifeboat Service was able to provide a lot of up-to-date information, but not all that we needed to know; so in October Captain Holter, Secretary-general of the service, went on a tour of inspection all along the coast of the West Country. He was able to fill in the gaps and this additional information was hurried to Shetland.

That autumn we had to deal with a number of drops of arms and instructors. One of the first was to be made over a place called Spalen, north of Oslo, and the code-phrase, "Nordmarka, where the people of Oslo seek their country air," was to be worked into the Norwegian news broadcast from London about 7:40 in the evening, to indicate that the drop would be made the following Tuesday, Wednesday, or Thursday, when certain light signals must be given from the ground. On another occasion, in mid-November, I had to go to Honefoss, a town forty miles to the northwest of Oslo, where the local resistance group was to be ready for three men with arms who were to be dropped four miles south of Aurdalsvann. The code word to be incorporated in the London news was "Sognefjorden." Again all went well.

Meanwhile, on October 24, 1942, Quisling had promulgated his new "law" confiscating the fortunes of Jews. Then, during the night of November 30 all male Jews over the age of fifteen were suddenly arrested to be sent to an extermination camp in Germany. We had learned of the shameful deeds of Quisling and his "government," but we had never thought they would perpetrate such a bastardly thing. It added impetus to Norwegian resistance to the Germans and our domestic Nazis. Even though the outlook looked as black and hopeless as ever, the resistance movement continued to gain ground. Churchill's announcement of the British victory at El Alamein made us feel better. Then the United States began its offensive against the Japanese in the Pacific, and for the first time we began to hope that the war might end.

At Christmas time in 1942 I paid a visit to Rjukan, mainly to learn about the big raids there on December 3. Apparently, the whole town had been searched. My parents' house had been gone over with a fine-toothed comb. Later, we discovered what had set this off. When some of the survivors of the glider group sent to destroy the heavy-water factory were caught, the Germans found a map disclosing that their objective had been Rjukan.

A few days after I left Rjukan, a school friend of mine there was arrested on suspicion of having taken part in the sabotage of the heavy-water factory. Later, I heard that the Gestapo had maltreated him appallingly, but that they got nothing out of him. My hatred for the Gestapo grew and grew as I heard how they had treated him and others like him, and that made me all the more determined to repay them.

CHAPTER IX

Hunted by the Gestapo

One of my contacts with 2 Group, a mason, had to leave his home
after a mysterious person twice telephoned asking for him. This made
us extra cautious, and when we learned that there was a possibility
that our friend had in his home the telephone number of a flat where
we often met, we decided to give up using the flat. It happened that a
couple of days later there were one or two things that I wanted to
check and this could only be done by going to the flat. As I approached
the building, it struck me that there was an unusual glow round the
blackout curtains, more than I had ever noticed before. At first I thought
it was my imagination, but even so I hesitated to approach the door.
Perhaps I ought to find a telephone and call first? In the end, I stifled
my doubts and hesitations and went inside, mounted the stairs, and
rang the doorbell. A second or two later the door was torn open and I
found myself staring into the muzzle of a pistol. The voice that told
me to come in was that of a Norwegian. Behind him I could glimpse
two other men. Involuntarily my hand moved towards the lapel of
my coat beneath which I had a pistol in a holster. The State Police
man came right up to me and pushed his pistol into my chest.

"Come inside at once!"

"Damned if I do," I shouted. I struck the gun aside and was down
the staircase and around the corner in nothing flat. Two shots were
fired at me, I suppose at about six feet, but it was dark and they missed.

A companion was waiting for me with a car. The engine started as I jumped in and off we sped. Perhaps they were bewildered. Whatever the reason, the three men in the flat did not seem to be chasing us. But then, of course, it was pitch dark. There seemed every chance that I had got away with it, and I was about to congratulate myself when I discovered something that I didn't like at all. As I had run out of the house, my briefcase had come undone and a large notebook had fallen out. As far as I could remember there was nothing dangerous or compromising in the notebook, but I was not sure.

I had to get it, but first I had to change my clothes. Obviously it wouldn't be safe to remain in the same grey military overcoat and fur cap I was wearing. I had other clothes in the house opposite the flat where the Germans were; so back I went. There were two entrances to this other building, neither visible from the windows of the flat with the Germans in it. I went in and was just about to start up the stairs when I heard shots and the sound of running feet. Something was up and the Germans obviously were there as well. I was only a few yards from the entrance, so I turned and hurried out again.

In this situation, I felt I just had to get that notebook; so taking a slightly firmer grip on the pistol, I walked straight to the house where I had just been shot at, through the gate, and along the side wall to the corner where I believed I dropped the notebook. There it was, lying on the edge of the banked snow. I picked it up and walked out through the gate again.

Later, I learned that Fehmer, the Gestapo man we feared most, had given this picture of the proceedings:

"As far as I could ascertain, Sonsteby came again to the flat after he and his companion escaped down the stairs. Sonsteby also went to the little house beside the filling station. The two men from the secret Field Police and the Norwegian constable were inefficient and he got away. Being afraid of getting into hot water, the three neglected to report this fact to their superiors, thereby making the effect of their mistake even more serious and hampering my search."

As soon as I could, I got in touch with Morland and Rivrud and we warned everyone who knew and used the two addresses. It had now become important for me to get hold of the mason and find out what had happened. It took me a couple of hours to locate him; then I went to see him.

The mason and a man from 2 Group had gone to the flat to meet a man at a certain time. The mason was on his guard because a day or two before he and I had a little experience, of which more anon, and as a precaution he had stuck a little pistol into the right-hand pocket of his overcoat. He had it in his hand as he rang the doorbell. Then the door was suddenly flung open and there stood three Germans shouting "Hands up!"

The mason reacted swiftly. He shot through the pocket of his coat, hitting two of the Germans. They collapsed and tumbled to the floor. The third German sent a spurt of bullets after the mason, as he and his companion rushed down the stairs and onto the street.

The whole incident depressed the mason considerably. Not that he grieved over the Germans he had shot but he feared the reprisals which the Germans usually indulged in after such an incident. But this was an idea we had to banish from our consciences. We couldn't give up the struggle because of possible innocent victims—a view which was shared by our superiors in London and Stockholm.

Our great advantage was that the Germans apparently did not know who had shot their Gestapo agents. Even so it was imperative to get the mason out of the country. We arranged that one of my Esso men and I should drive him to Kongsvinger in a big Esso tank-truck as soon as there was a favorable opportunity.

The next day was quite normal, but the following one brought disturbing news, which caused me to telephone Mrs. Andersen at the bakery. The moment she answered I got the impression that all was not well there. Later, I learned that the Germans had come there at eleven o'clock the previous evening. Mrs. Andersen had opened the door and had seen a number of Germans standing outside. They had asked for Reidun, the Andersens' daughter, and Mrs. Andersen had to admit that she lived there. The Germans thrust past her, arrested Reidun, and took her to Gestapo headquarters, where she was interrogated for nearly five hours.

We discovered later that the Germans had made a great round-up that night, especially of Communists, but they had also taken several of our people too. They had made about two hundred arrests.

First the baker's daughter was shown a photograph of a man she had seen at her home on various occasions who called himself Berg. Then the Germans held up a largish picture, turned with the back of it facing her, and when they suddenly turned it around, she found herself starring at my picture. However, she denied all knowledge of anyone they showed her and in the end she was sent to Grini Prison, from which, strangely enough, she was released after three months. The Germans had been unable to find anything that compromised her. Before that, however, while she was still at Gestapo headquarters on that eventful night, something happened that made the blood run cold in her veins. At the end of her interrogation as she was being taken away, she saw Halvor Rivrud and T. Aarnes being brought in and made to stand against a wall with their hands above their heads.

The Germans, having at last discovered my true name and identity, had gone at once to my flat at Therese Street, where they found and straightway arrested the two men who were living there. We learned later that they were horribly abused during their interrogation. We got this information from a man who had been in the same cell as Aarnes, but had been released and gone to his home in Drammen, outside Oslo. We heard of him through a contact we had in the prison itself, and I then got my mother, who could do this sort of thing more discreetly than we, to go and see him. He told her that Aarnes had been interrogated for four or five hours and had then been dumped on the floor of the man's cell, bloody and unconscious.

The following is Aarnes' own account of his interrogation: "I was taken for interrogation a few days after Halvor and I were arrested in January, 1943. At one o'clock I was taken up to the first floor (of 19 Moller Street where we were imprisoned) and up to a cell door. When the door was opened, I saw three men standing inside the room. I also noticed a small table with a typewriter on it. Before the door had shut behind me, one of the three jumped forward and took a firm grip on my throat. He pulled me forward into the middle of the floor and squeezed my throat harder. At the same time one of the others took up a position behind my back. This had a shock-effect on me, and I realized that it would be impossible to give the more or less plausible answers to their questions that I had been endeavoring to work out ever since we had been arrested. I had suddenly landed in an utterly unreal world.

"I had no breath, then the grip on my throat relaxed, and the first question came. I replied that I didn't know anything and was dealt a blow in the face. Almost simultaneously I was struck on the back of the head by the man behind me. Then came the second question, and my reply that I didn't know was instantly followed by another two blows. So it went on. The questions were in either German or Norwegian. All three men took active part. They bellowed and hit and kicked and were all around me. One of them used a sort of strap to strike me with, and another in his fury tore off his galoshes and hit me with those. They worked themselves into a state of frenzy, when they foamed at the mouth and looked pretty ugly. When my blood spurted into their faces, as it did at times, it only seemed to increase their frenzy. I gradually fell into a bemused state and my whole body was half numbed.

"I have no idea how many times I lost consciousness. Every time I came to, I was lying on the floor, with the three men running round me like wild beasts roaring at me to get up. If I didn't get up quickly enough, I was dragged up by the hair and placed on a chair. As soon as I had more or less come to my senses they resumed their maltreatment of me, but each time it took less to lay me out again.

"Eventually they stopped. One of them, who was the leader (I later discovered that his name was Hohler) then said something to me in German, the gist of which was:

" 'Torture is like a symphony. It has several movements. You have now experienced the first movement. Tonight, at Victoria Terrace, you will experience the second and third, and we shall get you to talk all right. We'll put screws on you, round your head and legs, and screw you to pieces.'

"After that I was led out into the passage, my face was washed and I was put against the wall, face turned to it, and there I stood for a couple of hours feeling most horribly depressed. At six or seven o'clock both Halvor and I were driven to Victoria Terrace, each handcuffed to a Gestapo man. I saw that Halvor's face was battered, so he must have had the same initial treatment as I. At Victoria Terrace I was put in a cell. Somewhere nearby, a radio was playing dance music, turned up as loud as it would go. Sitting there I began to feel horribly uncertain and afraid that I shouldn't be able to keep silent, if they started on more refined methods of torture.

"Several hours passed and nothing happened. About midnight, two Gestapo men came for me, but instead of being taken and interrogated, I was led to a car and driven back to Moller Street."

We could get no further direct news of the second man, Rivrud, but gathered that, if possible, he had a worse time of it than Aarnes.

A telephone call to Therese Street revealed that the Germans were still sitting there waiting, so Michelsen, with whom I worked closely, went into hiding. As for myself, the Germans now knew my name, but what of it? I just had to adapt to the fact and carry on. It wasn't pleasant to think of what might happen to my parents at Rjukan but, when mother and I discussed this aspect of the business, she assured me that I must carry on. If my parents went to Sweden for safety, the Germans would just go for my sister and her husband and family, if they wanted victims, so mother and father preferred to stay where they were.

The same night Rivrud, Aarnes and baker Andersen's daughter Reidun were arrested, the wife of the mason, Sverre Ellingsen, was taken as a hostage. She was sent to Grini, but fortunately she was released after a while. How she had come into it was this: A man had telephoned her and said that he absolutely must meet Ellingsen and asked that Ellingsen call a certain number to arrange a meeting. Ellingsen and I discussed this and decided that he ought to call the number. The man had told him that he had been under arrest at Moller Street and released and had messages for Ellingsen and a lot of information that would be of interest to our organization.

The more we discussed it, the more we smelled a rat. On the other hand, if the man was an *agent provocateur* and an informer, it would be important for him to make contacts. In that case it would be unlikely that the Germans would strike at his first meeting with us. Rather they would wait for him to obtain some measure of our confidence.

Eventually, we decided to meet Monsen, as he called himself, and arranged a rendezvous for eight o'clock in the evening at the Bear Fountain at Majorstue. At that hour it would be pitch dark. We went armed and we had a car parked close by with its engine running.

The man's appearance did not invite confidence. There was something queer about his eyes. After talking with him for a few minutes and arranging another meeting, neither Ellingsen nor I were in doubt: The man was an informer, a traitor.

And so he was. The Gestapo Chief, Fehmer, told one of his subordinates that he had managed to put one of his agents on a track that might perhaps lead to the capture of Sonsteby. This agent of his, a Norwegian, to whom he gave the cover name Monsen, was to meet

Sverre Ellingsen, whom the Gestapo knew to be a close collaborator of Sonsteby, and he added: "It's my intention to find out if he, Ellingsen, is still in touch with Sonsteby, before we arrest him. The main thing is to catch Sonsteby. So we are going to let this meeting between the two be watched, because I know from experience that these resistance people are very cautious and will smell a rat if they notice anything unusual in the vicinity."

After the meeting with us, Monsen went straight to Fehmer and reported everything. From his description Fehmer realized that it was I who accompanied Ellingsen. We did not, of course, go to the second meeting with Monsen.

Three days later I put on a white coat and got beside my Esso man, who sat at the wheel of one of the big Esso tank-trucks. The tanker had a locker at the rear in which the pipes used for discharging gasoline were stored. This compartment could be locked. We removed the pipes, Ellingsen crept inside, we locked him in and drove off towards Kongsvinger.

We got to Kongsvinger without incident. Ellingsen emerged and he and I went to Engebretsen, while the Esso man drove the tanker back to Oslo. Ellingsen and I then went on along the normal route, crossed the frontier safely, and were soon in Stockholm.

In Stockholm I was able to relax for a few days, enjoying the feeling that I didn't have to look around every street corner. Then, after a check up and a briefing, I took the train for Arvika and so across to Kongsvinger and Oslo. Controls were now a good deal stricter and it was a great satisfaction to present papers and an identity card I had made myself and get away with it. I don't think I looked like a suspicious character, and I was quite confident with my frontier-zone pass made out in the name of Nordstrand, timber-loader. No one could find anything wrong with that.

CHAPTER X

The Gestapo Strikes

When I returned to Oslo I heard that a couple of our men had been arrested at Bogstadsveien 53 and, alas, also the owner of the flat. The gas station attendant across the street had been taken too. But that was all that had happened. It looked as though Rivrud and Aarnes had managed to get through their interrogations without giving anything away. We felt able to take things calmly, though Michelsen remained in hiding for a while. Then unfortunately, Rivrud and Aarnes were sent to Germany.

I found myself a new hideout—with one of the doctors at the Gynecological Clinic. Through this doctor I met the Reverend Dagfinn Hauge, one of those who distributed the food parcels from Denmark. A certain proportion of these had been set aside for hospitals, but apparently not all were needed and some of the surplus began to go to our underground organizations. In fact we got so much that we had to find a warehouse for it, and my good caretaker who stored our radio and other equipment found us a good friend of his, also a caretaker, who let us have a whole cellar in "his" building.

Another person whose services we lost at this time was Henry Overby, a radio operator whom I had worked with. At five o'clock in the morning of January 8 some Germans armed with machine guns trooped up to his parents' flat where he was living. Fortunately the Germans had not noticed that there was a back entrance to the flat, and

Overby managed to sneak out that way and escaped under their very noses. However, they arrested his sister and she was jailed in Grini Prison.

Overby had been doing quite a lot with the naval group. At this time my contact with Milorg was Kai Holst, known to us as Kaka. I also used to meet Ole Borge who was to become "O", the Chief of Staff of the Central Leadership of Milorg. In fact, we now had numbers of contacts with Milorg and its subdivisions: intelligence, armament, supply and the ordinary hunter-groups up and down the country. Of course, this was not good security, but we were pretty well trained in our clandestine work and the dangers of compromising each other were less than one might have thought. The accident factor remained, of course, and I took up with various people the risk of sheer mischance compromising us all. Their argument was that, now that I was so badly wanted by the Germans, I ought to get out of the country. In principle, I agreed, but I wanted to carry on till the long days returned—till May or June.

What could the Germans have got out of me, if I had been caught? Actually, not such a lot. I met my people at tram stops, street corners, in parks, in various streets, in endless neutral places—banks, shops—and had no idea where they lived or worked. But I did know many of their proper names and so I was a bit of a threat.

When, by the end of January, the wave of arrests had not brought any further serious consequences, we felt that the interrogations were over and that we had got off pretty lightly. At the same time, it was obvious after the German defeat at Stalingrad and in Libya, that their controls and security would become much tighter.

Then, on February 23, I had a message from Rjukan that my father had been arrested. My mother had gone to Notodden, a town seventy miles to the south, to attend her mother's funeral. At eight o'clock that morning my father had gone to the basement, where my sister, who occupied the ground floor with her husband, was doing her washing. He said he was sorry to interrupt her, but thought he ought to tell her that the Germans wanted him to accompany them to Grini prison, so he couldn't very well say when he would be back.

As chance would have it, mother saw father on her way home. He was at Mael Station waiting for the ferry to take him across Tinnsjo, the usual way to Oslo. It was a hard blow for her. First, the anxiety about me, now this. She took it very well, was calm and controlled, and went to Oslo herself as soon as she could—and there we unexpectedly ran into each other. I explained that I hadn't yet managed to get out of the country, but was just about to go.

Michelsen had scarcely come out of hiding and gone back home, before the Gestapo struck. On March 19, at half past three in the morning, eight men appeared at his flat and went through it, but didn't find the secret hiding place under the dresser. At six o'clock they left, taking Michelsen with them, but leaving his wife. As soon as she felt the coast was reasonably clear, she got to work. She had to empty the hiding place and get out of the house the secret records, arms and a portable transmitter they had in the cellar before the Germans came back to make a more thorough search. The Michelsens had a young lodger, a girl from Rjukan, and the two women packed everything into a couple of trunks. At eight o'clock, two hours after the Germans had gone, they carried the trunks—Mrs. Michelsen was pregnant!—to a grocer's shop, some quarter of a mile away. The shop was owned by people who she knew would help her and look after the things.

Pregnant though she was, Mrs. Michelsen was turned out of her flat personally by Gestapo Chief Fehmer some time later. What she went through then caused her to be paralyzed for six months after giving birth to her daughter in November, 1943. After repeated interrogations, her husband was sent to Germany, where he died in Sachsenhausen in July, 1944.

The same night that the Gestapo arrested Michelsen, they also took the brothers Haga, who had sheltered various agents from England, and paid a visit to Marie Ek, my mother's closest friend in Oslo with whom I had lived frequently after the arrest of Aarnes and Rivrud in Therese Street. As it happened, Mother was staying with Mrs. Ek at the time and was able to tell me this:

At three o'clock in the morning three Gestapo men stormed into the flat, pistols drawn and ready. They searched the whole place. In one of the bedrooms were Mrs. Ek's lodgers, two brothers called Hille. They were questioned about what they knew of Gunnar Sonsteby and whether he had lived in the flat. They denied any knowledge. But when the Germans asked if he hadn't been there often, they felt they had to admit that he had spent one night there a long time before.

Mrs. Ek and mother were then questioned by Fehmer in person, who told mother that her son was a dreadful criminal. To this she replied:

"My son is not a criminal."

The Gestapo soon saw that there was little to be got out of that flat or those in it. There was a rather notorious Norwegian with them. He took my mother aside and said:

"I am a Norwegian. You can tell me all right, Mrs. Sonsteby. Your son's in Sweden now, I suppose."

Mother did not fall into that little trap.

"I'm sorry, but I don't know where he is."

The Germans took Mrs. Ek as a hostage and put her in Grini, where she remained until the end of the war.

It was about four o'clock when the Germans left, leaving mother feeling very insecure and expecting them back at any moment to fetch her. The worst of it was that I had arranged to come and see her at nine o'clock that morning. She took it into her head that if only she could get word to Mrs. Andersen at Gronland Street, the message might reach me in time to stop me.

For a while she racked her brains what to do. She was convinced that the Germans had put a guard on the house and that she stood no chance of getting out. She gave up the idea of trying to stop me from coming and wrote a letter to her sister at Notodden telling her what had happened. She put the letter in an envelope, stamped it, and then just threw it out of the window in the hope that the letter would reach its destination. So it did, a couple of days later. Some kindly soul had found the letter and posted it.

It was now about half past five and mother once again changed her mind and decided she must try to warn me after all. The Germans had taken most of her outdoor clothes with them when they left with Mrs. Ek, but she found an old overcoat and put this on over her nightdress. Then she stole downstairs and onto the street. Outside, there wasn't a soul to be seen, but she could not feel safe. Trying to act as though everything was perfectly normal, she went by the strangest and most devious ways to the East Station, where she walked about for a bit trying to make out whether she was being followed. When she finally decided that the coast was clear, she hurried to Gronland Street and Mrs. Andersen. The distance was only four blocks, or five to seven minutes' walk, but by trying to throw off imaginary pursuers she took a good hour to cover it.

Mrs. Andersen did not know where I was to be found, but she did know my taxi driver's telephone number and rang him. He managed to get the number of my hideout and the news reached me in time to stop me from keeping my nine o'clock appointment with mother.

In all probability the Germans had been so disappointed at the meager return from their visit to Mrs. Ek's flat that they had crossed it off their list for the time being, and I don't believe they had put any watch on it.

I told my mother that I was leaving in two or three days and would write to her as soon as I got to Stockholm. I didn't of course. I kept to my former plan, but I wrote her a letter which was taken to Stockholm and from there sent to an agreed contact in Rjukan. After she got this, mother felt more or less at ease about me. She still had father to think about—and he was in Grini.

Then my friends in the police told me point-blank that I must get out. I told them that I would—in a little while—and promised to be over the hills and far away in May, when the long days were at hand again. So I kept going for another month, avoiding all danger spots and never sleeping in the same place two nights in succession. Then on April 12 I took the old familiar route to Sweden, promising myself that I would be back in the autumn when the nights were long and dark again.

Before this, our main courier, Juden, had been arrested by the Swedes and had now got himself to England. The courier service had been altered, so that those from Stockholm only went as far as the frontier. The whole business was not a game with the Swedish frontier guards. On my way across on this occasion I had a meeting with officers from the Swedish Defense Staff and made arrangements for the provision of information from Norway, especially the frontier zone. I also tried to get a definite agreement for free passage for our couriers on our routes. They wouldn't promise anything, but we never had any more trouble or interference.

Once across the frontier I went to the customs officer at Hovildsrud-säter, and then the sheriff from Charlottenberg came and fetched me.

CHAPTER XI

In Sweden and England

I prepared to spend the summer in Sweden. It was interesting being in Stockholm and seeing the work from that end, though I soon got tired of hanging about waiting. Daniel Ring had gone to England and the office was now being run by Sverre Ellingsen. It had moved to the Norwegian Militaerkontoret, though it still came under the British—that is to say, SOE. At the beginning of 1942 a number of changes had been made in the Norwegian organization in Great Britain. A special Department (FO4) had been set up to deal with everything to do with the Resistance Movement in Norway, which for practical purposes meant Milorg. At the same time considerable changes were made in the relations between the Norwegians and SOE, which was a big organization working with the underground and resistance movements in all occupied countries, a collaboration committee being set up. As the Norwegian Resistance organization became more comprehensive, it had become difficult for the agents SOE sent from London to Norway to operate without coming up against Milorg. I knew from my own experience how easy it was for misunderstanding to arise and how easily these could prove dangerous for our resistance groups. It was also natural that those in Norwegian Independent Company No. 1 wanted to feel that all that they did in Norway was accepted by the Norwegian authorities. The early policy of separate Norwegian and British operations had been changed in favor of cooperation. The

British of course, had to have the say in Great Britain, and everything had to be organized from there, including the transport of agents to Norway by boat or plane. There had to be liaison and coordination in the work of the different organizations and this became closer as the years went by.

In Stockholm I met the head of our Militaerkontoret and a colonel from London, the head of FO4 who had come over to achieve closer contact with Milorg. I was asked my impression of Milorg and I had to tell him that in the summer and autumn of 1941 it had seemed hopeless to try to run a clandestine military organization in Norway, as though the time were not yet ripe for such a thing. Fatal mistakes had been made and severe losses suffered—but valuable experience had been gained and lessons learned, and I had considerably more faith in the idea now. Knut Moyen had built up an efficient nucleus and I believed that the thing was possible now. Moyen's successor, Hauge, was doing splendidly. He had the same great security sense and I had the best impression of him and his work. I told them I thought it was an advantage to have civilian chiefs for Milorg; if only because they were not so likely to be suspected by the Germans, who undoubtedly kept a sharp eye on all of high military rank. Moreover, it was hard for regular officers to get away from the professional way of thinking and they had no experience in a clandestine organization.

I told the colonel of my plans to wait in Sweden until late in August and then go back to Oslo and continue my work there. I realized that it might not be easy to stay so long in Sweden. The Swedes thought I had left the country long before in one of the "stay-put" boats, and it wouldn't be pleasant if I were interrogated under a different name. Of course, in those brutal times, Swedish jails were little more than a joke for us Norwegians, but I hoped it wouldn't come to that. Both our intelligence service and the Militaerkontoret were on a much better footing with the Swedes, and that could make things easier for me.

As before, I found that individually the Swedes were all right. I had several good friends among them and many helpers, but I never could understand the official Swedish attitude.

The colonel from London suggested that I go back with him to England. His idea was that I could join the Norwegian Independent Company, be trained and then sent back to Norway. I liked the idea, but I wanted a guarantee that I would be sent back to Norway as soon as my training was over. Or, if I couldn't get into the Independent Company, could I get into the Air Force? I was still only twenty-five. There could be no actual guarantee, but the colonel promised his help.

I was a little hesitant to go to England. I could foresee difficulties in getting back to Norway in the autumn if I was on the wrong side of the North Sea, and I wanted several days to think about it. I had, of course, heard of the fantastic training our men got when they went to England and I was eager to have that. I had been impressed by the English-trained men whom I had come across, so finally I decided to accept the offer.

In order to get away, I had to have a Norwegian passport and the simplest way of getting one was to go back to the frontier and report to the authorities as a refugee, using a suitable name. I had been once or twice in Gothenburg and had some friends there I wished to see, so I decided to go there and so on to Strömstad—on the coast a dozen miles from the frontier—and go to the police there and say I was a refugee.

I arrived in Strömstad in the evening of April 20, dressed in Norwegian clothes except for a Swedish overcoat and hat. I had a Swedish suitcase containing a Norwegian cap and an old overcoat I had found at a clothing center for refugees in Gothenburg. Some Norwegian refugees must have left their old things there when they had been given new Swedish ones. The first thing I did was to go for a walk along the river (I had been in Strömstad on bicycle trips before the war and remembered it) and in the dark there I took the cap and coat from my suitcase and put them on. Then I stuffed the Swedish hat and coat into the suitcase and chucked it into the river. After this little camouflage-maneuver, I went to the police station and told them that I had been put ashore by a boat from Tonsberg. When they wanted to go into details, I told them I couldn't say more for fear of causing difficulties for people still in Norway.

I had a fake identity card in the name of Erling Fjeld and that was the name I used. All went well, and the following day I was sent with some others to the reception center for Norwegian refugees. Here I quickly got in touch with the military representative and was sent to Stockholm. All was now clear and I left on May 9, 1943.

I was happy but not feeling too well, for on my trip to the frontier I had contracted a nasty case of tonsilitis which had sent me to bed for several days and I had only just got up. Thus although it was my first flight, that trip was anything but pleasant. The plane flew at a great height and in complete darkness. It was very cold. We arrived at Leuchars near St. Andrews without incident in the early hours. The Swedes had stamped my passport in the normal manner before we left Bromma, the Stockholm airport, so there was no hold-up as far as I was concerned. The next stage was to London by train, with a British SOE officer as an escort.

I thought that all was now over or if there was to be any more, it would all be clear sailing; but instead I found I had yet to pass through the eye of the needle—the British security services' organization for screening foreigners. This was done at the Royal Victoria Patriotic School, and there I was examined (dissected would have been a good description of the procedure), and the whole thing was something of a nightmare. It was my first visit to England, and evidently the British were not going to accept me until they were one hundred per-cent sure of me. They asked about everything under the sun in Norway and laid so many traps that I realized how difficult it would have been for an *agent provocateur* to slip through. Hundreds of Norwegians had passed through the school before me—many of them with personal experience and knowledge of the underground work being done in Oslo—and my examiners were perfectly familiar with conditions there. But I was able to tell them a thing or two as well, and after four days of questioning they had done with me.

There were people from all over the world at the school: Negroes from Africa, Frenchmen, Belgians, Rumanians, Hungarians, etc. I had to sleep in that gigantic dormitory along with forty or fifty others. The room was hellishly hot and the men just seemed to lie in their beds smoking.

Things were difficult for the British at the time, especially for the Londoners. London had been badly bombed and, everything considered, we at the school were pretty well off.

I was let out on May 17 and got in contact with the Norwegian authorities and some of my friends, and we had a reunion at the Cumberland Hotel. The first thing I had to do, of course, was to introduce myself anew to my friends, under my new name. Then after various medical examinations and interviews I was accepted for military service and for special duties.

I was now Private Fjeld of the Norwegian Forces in the United Kingdom. According to my Soldier's Book I was born on January 3, 1916, and was to serve for the "duration." How long would that be? Well, that wasn't my headache. I had joined the darned thing and must take what was coming.

At the beginning of June, I and some twenty-five or thirty others were sent north by train from London to a Special Training School at a secret destination. After a couple of days we found ourselves near the west coast of Scotland, in desolate country north of Fort William. We were installed in a big house near the sea not far from the villages of Arisaig and Mallaig.

I wasn't feeling very well. My legs hadn't properly recovered from the frostbite and I dreaded the idea of special training. I ought to have had a longish holiday before being sent on a Commando Course. However, there was no mama to run to there, and I just had to get on with it. In fact, I had hardly got my new boots on before I was sent out on a strenuous route march and run, seven miles along roads—just as a beginning! After that I tried to take things quietly, but this decision was not at all well received by the officer in charge. Now discipline has never been my strong suit, so this captain and I didn't exactly see eye to eye. But the sun was shining, there wasn't a cloud in the sky, we were out in the open air all day long and it was a good time in every way. The men there were very fine fellows. My best friend was Erling Lorentzen, and often we sat on the mountainside discussing the future—mostly the immediate future as it concerned us: What jobs we would be assigned in Norway.

For some inexplicable reason, the subject that interested me most was explosives, and I really think I was a good pupil, even if the captain didn't. He had rather got my back up and I could never resist any chance to make a fool of him. It became an absolute sport as far as I was concerned.

I acquired a number of curious accomplishments and learned many strange things. Also I became fit again. Great weight was attached to guerrilla training and, although I tried to pick up as much as possible, I could never believe that I was going to have use for all that we learned. But then many of the others might easily be going on missions where it would all be useful. The special problems and requirements of resistance work, I took it, would be dealt with in a further course at the Norwegian Independent Company's main camp on the East Coast.

The others were amused by the strained relations between me and our captain, and this made me worse. One day at the rifle range I really went too far. When the markers were up at the targets, a shot rang out and a bullet from my rifle sped over the markers' heads towards the sheep on the hillside beyond. The reaction was immediate and sharp. I was given a tremendous ticking off, ordered back to quarters, and told I would be posted. I had no idea that this, and other things, would make complications for me. I had assumed our group was fairly "tough" and not expected to be under such strict military discipline. Another far from exemplary pupil was a man I knew from Resistance work in Oslo, a shipping man from Kristiansand, Viggo Axelssen. It was he who initiated the report that started the chase after the *Bismarck*.

The officer in charge of training was within his rights, of course. He wasn't very familiar with the Norwegian character and temper and took a professional soldierly view of his job. His pupils, however, were going to operate behind the enemy's lines as saboteurs. Their training could only be general. There were people of all nationalities on successive courses, and the staff had no time for such niceties as considering the psychology of individuals.

We learned a lot and did a lot. The commando runs we had to do were pretty hard. We became a well-trained gang, and the instructors laid the foundations of that spirit which imbued all the agents from Britain I had met. I was impressed by our shooting training, particularly the so-called instinctive method of firing a double shot. This was designed to break down the opponents, morale, and it did have a real effect.

In the end I realized that the captain couldn't stand me. At this juncture, all the others had been allowed to act as leaders during an exercise.

Then Colonel J. S. Wilson, head of the Scandinavian Section of SOE came up from London. I didn't know that he made the trip because the officer in charge of the course training was trying to get rid of me. Later, Wilson told me that, although he had initiated the whole SOE Training Scheme in 1940, he had always held that the people in the Training Section were not to select candidates or have the final judgment of them. This was the responsibility of the Country Section. My case thus became a test, and Wilson fought for me as hard as he could—and won.

As I learned later, the captain was told to allow me to lead an exercise like the others. For some strange reason mine was the concluding exercise of the course, in which we all took part instead of being divided into two parts as had been done before. A certain area, supposed to be an aerodrome, was to be captured. Exact plans had to be worked out, and the theory behind it propounded and discussed. I had not paid great attention to theory, but here Erling Lorentzen came to my aid. He was still only twenty and the youngest person there; but he had been a good and attentive pupil and he knew it all. He helped me with sketch maps and dealt with the theoretical part of the task.

There was a definite pattern that everything should have followed, but we had a rather original idea. There was an old narrow-gauge trolley railway there, which had been used to transport building material or something. We managed to find a trolley and haul it up to the top of the hill. Our idea was that, during the actual attack, we should get onto the trolley and sweep down the line to our objective, the aerodrome. We reckoned that the trolley would not be able to take the last bend, but would go off the rails there, and before that happened we were to jump off at high speed. We had a lot of fun with the idea of it and thought it a wonderful way of making our debut. It was a wonder we didn't break our legs when we jumped off. The attack went according to plan and I thought we acquitted ourselves pretty well, though perhaps our instructors weren't quite as pleased as I.

After this we were to be sent to a parachute-jumping course. A few were not put down for this course, including Viggo Axelssen and myself. We realized that we hadn't been found suitable for further service in Norwegian Independent Company No. 1 and, in spite of everything, thought it a bit unfair that we should be kicked out like that, just because we hadn't behaved. It wasn't school conditions that awaited us in Norway, if we were going to be sent back there. However, we felt that we could count on our friends in London. They knew us better.

How and why things were finally decided as they were I never discovered, but I was posted to NORIC's Depot in Invernessshire and Axelssen was sent to the Navy to serve in our motor-torpedo boats. It wasn't long, however, before this was rectified and he came back to NORIC and was eventually sent to Oslo.

Most of the instructors at Drumintoul were Norwegian, though they worked under the British. Many of them were outstanding. Most of them had experience with the work and conditions in Norway, and that was a tremendous advantage. Here I met Joachim Ronneberg and others of the famous heavy-water operation and the advance party that had gone to Hardanger Vidda to prepare the action. They were both there as instructors, and they certainly knew what they were talking about.

Again it was explosives that I found the most interesting. Day and night we practiced laying charges in all sorts of places and calculating how much explosive we should need to accomplish various tasks—especially of the so-called plastic explosives, which acted very differently from dynamite.

My old friend Knut Haugland, who had been radio operator for the heavy-water action, was preparing to go back to Norway to help organize liaison. He was to be of great help to me.

I came to London at the end of September and began to worry about getting back to Norway. It was complicated business equipping an expedition. And was it really so important for the British and Norwegians to get me home? I had worked in the Resistance there for two or three years, but I was far from the only one. And what jobs were they envisaging for me in my proper area: Oslo and surroundings? The fact that I had been SOE's agent there cut no ice in England, and my work was being done perfectly by Morland and his helper. I began to feel depressed. The prospect of getting back was dwindling.

Knut Haugland came to my aid. He had gathered from Norwegian Dept. 4 and Colonel Wilson that it was not going to be easy to organize a flight just to get me back, and Haugland got the splendid idea that I should go as his assistant on his liaison expedition. He needed someone to help him set up his transmitter in Oslo—preferably someone who knew his way about.

Haugland's plan was well received by both British and Norwegians, and soon the signal was green for my return. I was to be the second member of Operation Curlew. I rejoiced, but too early.

There was still one important question to be answered: Would I be able to remain in Oslo? They couldn't forget that I was wanted and some people doubted whether it was right to send me back at all. So, once again I was interrogated by my fellow countrymen, in particular by an old acquaintance, Otto Berg, with whom I had travelled from Stockholm to Oslo in 1942. He was attached to Chief of Police's Intelligence Bureau and acted as FO4's consultant in checking their agents. Berg was now instructed to prepare an exhaustive report on my activities in Norway. I was to be screened as well as possible before they let me go back. The thing was that a number of those with whom I had been in contact in Norway had been arrested, and it was possible that I might be a German spy. I didn't know this of course, nor was there any suspicion of it, but they thought it correct to make a thorough investigation. Naturally, I was not shown Berg's report at the time. The following was his conclusion:

> Up to this point there has been nothing about Sonsteby's way of working or his methods within the underground organization that one can criticize. Nor can it be said that anyone's arrest has been due to lack of caution on his part. As will be apparent from the report, Sonsteby has always arranged his work on liaison lines and he has been forced to meet numbers of people, yet few know or have known his true name. He has been careful to change residence continually, not to have any permanent employment or place of business where he could be found, and thus, even if his illegal activities have been known to the Gestapo, it has been impossible to catch him. This latter fact, in particular, ought to carry considerable weight in assessing the importance Sonsteby's knowledge of leading members of the organization would have if he were sent home. A certain skepticism about the rightness of sending him back is understandable, just because of this background and his personal knowledge and the results it might have for the Home Front if he were to be captured by the Germans, but one must not forget his cleverness and astuteness during those years. I can see no

reason why Sonsteby should not be used for the mission for which he has been chosen, but I fully understand the objections that can be made to the project. Let me also say that my point of view may be influenced by Sonsteby's personality and thus may be prejudiced to a certain degree.

This report of Berg's gave me the final all clear and the project then went to the British. A telegram was sent to Oslo asking the heads of Milorg for their opinion. Milorg replied that they would be glad to see me back.

The British attitude toward Milorg and its chiefs was very different now, and so was that of the Norwegian civil and military authorities in London. Milorg had finally obtained the recognition it deserved and, with Hauge following in Moyen's security-footsteps so well, it looked as though it were in very healthy shape. Also, the position now was that agents from UK, the boys from NORIC 1, could not operate on their own, but had to cooperate with Milorg and so they were eventually put under Milorg.

I had now been to the parachute school at Manchester and made my jumps, three from a plane and two from a balloon, one at midnight. We had been tremendously impressed by one of the men at that school. He had refused to jump from the plane. If we had done as in our heart of hearts we wanted to do, we would have refused too, but I suppose we didn't have the courage to do that. It was bad enough jumping out into space; it called for even greater moral courage to stay in the plane and let it fly back with one. All had gone well and I now considered myself well enough trained to be parachuted into Norway.

My legs had quite recovered and I felt as fit as when I first began in 1940.

CHAPTER XII

Parachuting into Norway

The important thing now was to get back to Norway as soon as I could, and after the trouble I had caused my chiefs in England I felt they would be glad to see me go. My admiration for the British was considerable, but I found it easy to contain it where one or two types were concerned. I was greatly impressed by Colonel J. S. Wilson, the former police chief of Calcutta, who was head of our section in SOE. I had a great respect for him and even stood a bit in awe of this taciturn man. He invited me to his home once or twice and there I met Shetlands Larsen, as he was then beginning to be called.

Knut Haugland was to take a certain quantity of equipment with him to Norway, including special explosives for destroying German communications in Norway. We were also to take two or three tons of arms for the Milorg forces south and west of Oslo. A group of Milorg people were to await us when we landed near a small cottage up on the Skrim plateau near Kongsberg. Another group of people with various assignments in Oslo were to be dropped at the same time. One or two members of this group had stayed in Norway after the last action and they were to come to Skrim with the Milorg people to receive us all.

Our equipment and supplies were ready by the beginning of October and we were sent to "Station 61" near Cambridge. Here, for security reasons, we were as good as interned in a huge country mansion standing all by itself in a large park. With me were men of all nationalities. Some had assignments in different European countries and there were those who were going to be dropped behind the German lines to do guerrilla or other resistance work. Some were destined for places as far away as Jugoslavia; others were going to Germany, Denmark, and Norway. The mood of the place was extraordinary. I have never known anything like it. We were waited on hand and foot; the food was first class and I had the impression that, as with men in death row, considerable weight was attached to making our last meal a really good one.

The days before our departure were divided between training and amusement. No one we talked with gave any information about his mission. Everything was top secret. Even the women who ran the house were in uniform and subject to strict control.

We had to wait until weather conditions were right. We could only jump over Norway in bright moonlight and with unobscured vision. Finally we took off from an aerodrome near our secret quarters on October 11 in a four-engined Halifax bomber. It was evening when we took off and by midnight we were passing the Norwegian coast at Flekkefjord, near the southern tip of the country. There was a magical element in this nocturnal reunion with our country, and we were impatient to make our jumps.

However, there was thick mist over the Skrim plateau and the pilot forbade the jump. He circled over Drammen and Oslo and dropped a number of leaflets. On the whole the German AA guns were not much in evidence. A few had fired at us as we crossed the coast, and also at Oslo, but nothing troublesome.

The bomber then turned west and headed for Scotland. We landed safely towards morning and later in the forenoon the plane took us back near Cambridge where we had started from.

On October 15 we took off again, and again we had to turn back when conditions proved hopeless. Twice, now, I had sat there ready to jump through the floor of the plane; it was even worse having to be taken back again. Some days later we went through the same experience—and again a fourth time. We were beginning to be fed up and disgruntled. Then the moon was wrong and we had to sit and wait for the next full moon—November 12.

On that day, we tried again. At first all went well, but when we

From the students' lodge, winter 1940. Sonsteby third from left, Knut Moyen and Mrs. Moyen to his left.

Knut Haugland saying goodbye to Mrs. Sonsteby before fleeing to Sweden.

Oscar Westby.

Sonsteby with customs officer Johan Ostlie and his wife, after the liberation.

Claus Helberg during the occupation, as a secret wireless operator in the Rjukan mountains.

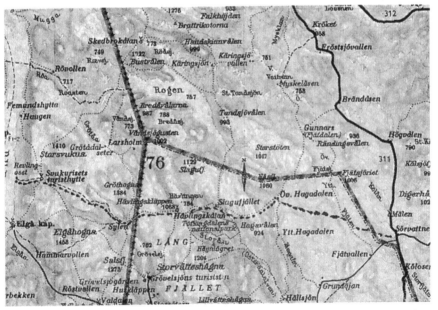

The trail used by Claus Helberg and Sonsteby to secretly cross the border of Sweden and Norway in order to reach the Femund Lake.

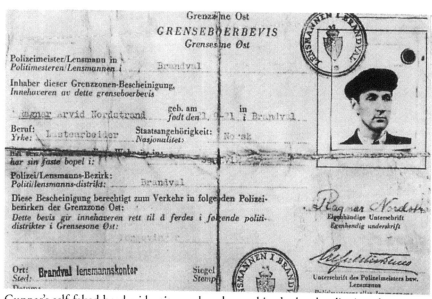

Gunnar's self-faked border identity card, to be used in the border district where passage was forbidden by patrolling Nazi forces.

"The Baker" Hans Anderson and his wife Liv Anderson with Sonsteby.

Reidun Anderson, daughter of "The Baker" Hans Anderson, in 1943.

Comrades in arms.

Albin Skoglund and his wife in Austmarka.

Alma and Emil Skogland on their farm, close to the border.

Gunnar on a visit to the Hakerudtomta farm after the war.

Some of the many false identity cards used by Sonsteby.

The entrance where the Gestapo waited to capture Sonsteby.

Gunnar's parents, Margit and Gustav
Sonsteby

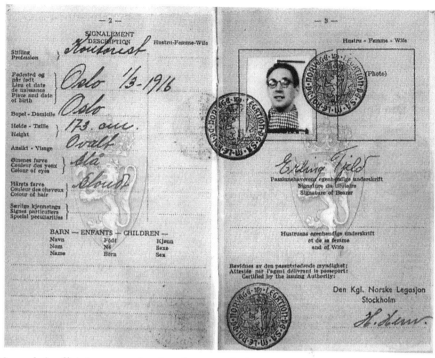

Sonsteby's official passport, bearing the name "Erling Fjeld."

Erling Fjeld's military identity card.

Knut Haugland as a Lieutenant in England.

Colonel John Skinner Wilson, later director of Boy Scouts International.

The Norwegian Independant Company's training ground in Scotland.

The gasoline tank car that caused all the trouble.

Thoralf Thorp.

The railroad bridge hindering the load of arms.

The labor office, destroyed.

From the attic window (A) the boys reach the building to attack.

Per Morland.

Gregers Gram, resting in neutral Sweden, 1944.

Sonsteby and Arne Gundeid at the first gate.

The 180-foot-long wall of the factory building, destroyed.

Inside the machine hall.

The turntable at Skabo.

Top secret visit from High Command in London. Colonel Oen in dark clothes.

Sverre Hornbaech, the taxi driver.

Jens Christian Hauge, the resistance leader.

The cover firm Holatex Ltd. on the top floor of the corner building.

Sonsteby's false identity card, depicting him as a secret federal Nazi police officer.

At the end of WWII, the sabotage of the Norwegian Railways building under Nazi command.

Gunnar as the leader of the bodyguard unit for the royal family. In the car with King Olav and his children, Ragnhild, Astrid and Harald, who today is King of Norway.

Sonsteby at King Haakon's farm outside Oslo. King Haakon in the chair.

were out over the North Sea, gasoline suddenly began to pour in to where we were sitting. Knut Haugland was rather ill that day, having contracted a gastric chill or something of the kind, and he was lying on the floor with a blanket over him. The stink of the gasoline trickling in was scarcely calculated to make him feel better. We wondered what on earth was up. The pilot did the only thing possible: He turned and headed for the nearest airport.

We were ten miles out from the coast at the time and it was essential to lighten the plane as much as possible to maintain height. So the pilot ordered us to jettison all our equipment. For us that was tragedy, but we had to obey. Knut had spent months getting all that magnificent equipment together, and now we had to dump it into the sea! We felt we would almost prefer to land on the water.

That, apparently, was a highly probable outcome even after the plane had been lightened, and we had to take off our parachutes and put on Mae Wests. We were told that if we landed on the water, we would, if we were lucky, have three or four minutes in which to get into the rubber dinghies. Anything can happen when you land in roughish seas, and the gasoline swishing about and forming pools on the floor might contribute its own surprises.

At last the coast appeared below and we could breathe more easily. The airfield at Snoring soon came into sight. The pilot had been in radio contact and we saw that the emergency stand-by had been ordered: ambulances and fire-engines and the lot. No doubt, when a plane landed soaking with gasoline that was all very necessary, or could be. However, we had no need of it. The plane landed without mishap and for the fifth time we were carted back to where we had started.

Five days later, on November 17, we were airborne once more. This time we got across the North Sea and were soon over Telemark. I was sitting beside the opening in the floor ready to jump as we crossed lake Norsjo at Notodden. At the command "Action Stations" we were to sit upright, legs over the edge of the hole, hands clamped to our sides and our feet close together, and at "Go" we had to shove off.

Our excitement was intense. It was a minute or two after two o'clock. I saw the lake under me. Then it was gone. Then came another lake, Myklevann, up on the plateau itself, and a few minutes later I caught sight of bog and moor beneath us and there at last the lights we were hoping to see. The captain gave the green light, the warning light came on beside me, I heard the words "Action Station," then "Go" and I jumped. The next instant, my face and body were buffetted by bitingly cold air. I plunged down at great speed gasping for breath, but before I had time to wonder whether the parachute was going to open or not, I felt a violent jerk and there I was hanging.

I realized at once that we had been put out far too high. It must have been nearer 2,000 feet than the 1,000 feet that had been planned. The force of the wind was carrying me sideways. I was struck by the magnificence of the view: In the distance I could see the river Lagen shining in the bright moonlight, and in the other direction I could see away back to Notodden and the mountains beyond.

I had been so occupied with my jump, that I hadn't looked to see how Haugland was doing. Now I saw several parachutes ahead of me and assumed that one of these must be Haugland's and the others those of the containers with our equipment. We were already a good distance from each other.

As I got nearer the ground, I caught sight of the little cottage that was our objective. I was about 300 feet above it then, with the wind sweeping me along towards some woods. Remembering what I had been taught at the Parachute School, I turned in my harness so I was facing the direction in which I was going, but I was carried on and on, and was soon sailing along above the treetops. I knew I could expect a good hard bump when I finally hit.

Once among the treetops, I held one foot out in front of me as a shock absorber, suddenly there was a great jerk as the parachute caught in a tree and, before I knew what had happened, I was hanging in my harness just a couple of feet off the ground. In a moment I had got out the knife I carried, cut the cords, and dropped into loose snow.

I had been lucky. My next job was to get my parachute down from the tree, fold it up, and hide it. That done, I took off my thick parachute suit and put it with the parachute. Then through snow to the hut, where I was met by our "reception committee," which included two others from England who had come in just ahead of us. Haugland turned up soon afterwards. He had made a good landing on snow-covered bog, a bit closer to the hut than I.

We soon found the container with skis which had been parachuted immediately after us, and in it were our rucksacks. The reception group told us we were going to have considerably more trouble gathering together the twenty or so containers with arms and equipment. They apparently were scattered over a vast area; and some might even have landed as far away as the Lagen valley, where the mountainside ended in a sheer drop. Altogether our two planes had dropped between thirty-five and forty parachutes. In the course of the day, we brought in the weapon containers and carefully camouflaged them with snow.

When Haugland made contact with London on his transmitter (which had the code name Tricorne Red), he was told to go as soon as possible to the local Milorg chief at Kongsberg, down in the valley and a few miles to the north. Filling his rucksack with equipment, he put on his skis and went off. At the first place he came to in the valley, he got a taxi to drive him to Kongsberg. Two days later to our surprise, he turned up again at the hut on the plateau, exhausted and very much the worse for wear. His face bore the obvious marks of blows.

What had happened was this: While Haugland was with the local Milorg man at Kongsberg, the Gestapo arrived and arrested everyone present. The Germans suspected that Haugland had come from England and naturally treated him with particularly loving attention. He was subjected to a true Gestapo interrogation, hence the marks on his face. When that was over and he and the Milorg man were being taken outside to the Germans' car, he managed to ease the straps of his rucksack almost off his shoulders and, as they reached the stairs, he let his rucksack drop and took a great leap down the stairs and out. Once in the street, he ran in the direction of the Arms Factory and from there into the woods. Thanks to a tiny compass which the Germans had overlooked, he made his way to the hut. We were overjoyed that he had escaped. The episode was duly reported to London.

The whole thing was most unfortunate for us, of course. It showed that the Germans were aware of the nocturnal air visits and there was a good chance that they knew that planes had been over the Skrim plateau. After a brief council of war we decided to leave the area.

I longed to get back to Oslo. I felt that the hut up there on the mountain might become a dangerous trap.

It was curious how different our mentalities were. Some of us were happiest in Oslo, where we knew conditions and felt at home. Others wanted to avoid Oslo and towns in general and would have preferred the woods and fields. Whatever our course, it was obvious that we had to get away from the area of the drop as quickly as possible.

So, at eight o'clock in the evening of November 25, 1943, we went down to the low road to meet the truck that was to take us to Horten on Oslo Fjord.

Till then the weather had been cold but clear; now it turned to rain and we huddled under some trees on the fringe of the woods as we waited. It seemed the lorry would never come, and tension mounted. Several hours late, it arrived. By then we were wet through and chilled to the marrow by the rain and sleet. The temperature had dropped to about 3° and it was a chattering, shivering band that climbed onto the open truck when it arrived. When we got near the coast, the group scattered. Some went to Tönsberg, Haugland to Andebu, and I and another went to Horten to spend the night. Martin Olsen had gone ahead to Oslo and was to come to Horten to fetch us and our equipment.

At Horten, we went to sleep on the floor of a friend's sitting room, feeling far from safe because there had been a lot of disturbing German activity in the town. When a car suddenly pulled up outside later that night, I and the man I was with scrambled into our clothes in a jiffy, ready to bolt. However, our visitor proved to be Olsen, who had got to Horten quicker than we had expected. Since he was there, we thought we might as well leave right away, so we got into the car and drove to Oslo.

CHAPTER XIII

Oslo - A Resistance Nest

It was like a fantasy being in Oslo again. The situation had not improved, of course, and many new arrests had been made. Per Morland had been working tirelessly to keep the organization together.

One of the first things I had to do was to find a good hideout for Haugland, somewhere where he could feel more or less secure. I spent a few days at the Gynecological Clinic where I had been in hiding before I went to England. It was agreed that Haugland should live there. Meanwhile, I would get myself a set of different places, which only a few of my contacts need know of.

I had reached Oslo just at the time of the Student Action. Hitler wanted to close the university and put the students in camps in Germany for a brainwashing. Nothing was achieved with some 1,200 who were sent, but what amazed and disappointed us was that not more of the students had the enterprise and initiative to escape, although they'd had ample warning and plenty of opportunity.

At the places where I spent my nights, I said I was a student in hiding. At one place, I made the same mistake I had once before, leaving my pistol under my pillow when I went out one morning, so perhaps they were not altogether convinced by my story.

Gradually I got in touch with a number of people anxious to work for us and made other useful contacts, including the discovery of a former schoolfriend in the state control board for gas generators. We had to have these ghastly generators on the cars we used and, as they weren't easy to get, he was a most useful friend at court. Apart from this, he was already working for our group and doing a good job, too.

One of the first things to be done after Haugland was installed at the Gynecological Clinic was to get his equipment and arms from Skrim. There was quite a lot of it and it obviously couldn't be transported in an ordinary open truck. It was reported to be well hidden in the valley. What with all the arms and ammunition and wireless equipment, there were a good two or three tons to be moved.

I consulted my friend the Esso man and we agreed that a tank truck was needed. So, early one cold winter's morning, we drove off in an Esso tanker out of Oslo, through Drammen, and on into the country to where the things were. Two of our men were there to help us. The business of unscrewing the five covers on the tanks was laborious, but within a couple of hours we had everything stowed inside the tanker.

We had to wait for darkness before we could drive back, and it was late before we got away. We followed our practice of returning by a different route; to do this we had to go under one or two low railway bridges where we weren't sure there would be enough headroom. Our fears were justified. When we got to the railway bridge at Skollenberg we stuck. There just wasn't quite enough room. Each of the five covers on the tanker had special circular knobs and it was these that were catching.

At eleven o'clock at night there were only two choices to be made: either we could let some air out of the tires so the tanker was not riding so high, or we would have to unscrew all five covers again. There proved to be no pump with the tanker and, as we didn't know how far it was to the nearest garage where we could blow the tires up again, we did not dare let the air out in case we ruined the tires. So, we had to take the covers off again. While we were at this laborious job, several cars passed us, including one full of German soldiers. They seemed to be most sympathetic and shouted encouragement. Fortunately, none of them took it into his head to climb up and have a look at our "gasoline."

It took us nearly an hour to get the covers off, drive the tanker through, and put the covers back. We proceeded to Oslo without further incident. Most of the equipment went to Milorg via Haugland; but part of the arms and explosive went to our own stores.

I was supposed to act as liaison between Haugland and SL (Central

Committee), but we felt it was best for me to get properly acclimatized first and to do this I took up my old work. I worked out my own program and didn't pay what one could call slavish attention to our operation orders. Why should I? I was in my old stamping ground —and out of London's reach. Perhaps it sounds as though I was stubborn and insubordinate, but I knew that until I felt sure of myself again I could not do a really useful job.

At this time I had no direct contact with my family. My father was still in Grini Prison, and mother was in Rjukan, though she came on visits to Oslo now and then. I tried to find out by devious ways when she was coming, to avoid running into her. She got letters from me regularly, however; they reached her from Sweden via a contact in Rjukan and she thought me safely in England.

At baker Andersen's in Gronland Street, all continued as before. We used the place with caution, but we still used it, and Mrs. Andersen and her daughter were as helpful as ever.

Our faithful taxi driver, Hornbaech, had had to give up his taxi. Its make and appearance had become too well known and would have given him away in any tight corner. Instead, he had got himself a small van which he could fit with false license plates and use for every kind of job. Hornbaech had arranged a signal code by which his wife could warn him of danger. These signals ranged from a certain flower displayed in the window to phrases to use in a telephone conversation. If his wife said their three-year-old had whooping cough, that meant danger.

On December 6, Hornbaech ran into difficulties. The next morning when he rang up his wife, she told him the child was whooping, so he knew things had really gone wrong. The Germans had been there but, not finding Hornbaech, had gone away again. When he learned of this, he took up a position near his home to await an opportunity to collect his family and take them all into hiding. However, the Germans returned before Mrs. Hornbaech had time to leave the flat.

Hornbaech himself was walking along the pavement near the entrance to his block when he saw a car pull up and three men jump out. He walked on as though nothing had happened and passed the three men without their noticing him. He saw them go into the building. He stopped at a distance to watch and saw his wife come out with their young daughter in her arms, followed by the Germans. It was a ghastly thing for any man to have to stand helplessly and watch. (Luckily, their elder child had managed to get away.)

The Germans then drove Mrs. Hornbaech to her mother's, with whom she left the three-year-old, but at Grini they threatened her that they would take the child away and send it to a home in Germany if she didn't answer their questions. It was a horrible time for both parents.

In the circumstances, it was decided that Hornbaech must go to Sweden.

Morland and I celebrated our fourth Christmas under German Occupation together. We paid visits to the Andersens at Gronland Street, to our doctor friend at the Gynecological Clinic, and then went to a farm north of Oslo. The people there were old friends from our Student Hut days, and it was a real holiday.

After Christmas we got busy. With Hornbaech gone, I had to find a new driver. Although I had been taught to drive a train at the school near Mallaig, I could not drive a car. Through the owners of one of my hideouts I made contact with an unemployed driver. I got hold of an Opel Olympia and mounted a small carbide-generator up behind. The fact that there was no connection between the generator and the engine was no concern to anyone but ourselves. It looked perfect.

I kept in touch with several of the NORIC men, including Stenersen and Martin Olsen. Shortly before Christmas—I think at the beginning of December—they had been surprised by the Gestapo in their flat. Martin Olsen managed to escape but Stenersen was wounded and arrested. I was given the job of contacting them in the prison itself. Through my old friend and helper Mrs. Collett, I got in touch with the Prison Chaplain, Dagfinn Hauge, and through him with the prison cook, a man called Gullerud. The first thing we did after that was to smuggle a cyanide pill to the wretched Stenersen, for him to use in an extremity. Gullerud had cleverly got a message to Stenersen asking him to keep a look out and wipe his window with a piece of rag when he saw the cook near and then drop the rag. Gullerud would then pick the rag up and give it back to him with the pill in it. All went well and the pill was passed successfully, but unfortunately Gullerud was seen to speak to Stenersen and that made the guards suspicious. He had to go into hiding a few days later, but not till he had got us keys to the main gate of the prison and even to Stenersen's very cell.

Having the keys, we made a plan to rescue Stenersen, who was one of NORIC's (Norwegian Independent Company) people and had a lot of valuable information. It was a daring plan and it might have come off, but unfortunately there was no time to try. Stenersen made a fantastic attempt to escape and was killed.

Just before Christmas a new group arrived from England to sabotage ships in Oslo harbor. We helped them find hideouts and supplies. We had a good contact who worked at the police garage and he was of great help to them.

All that spring our little group continued its work, which was becoming more and more varied. I had more and more to do with Milorg's central organization and its chief, Hauge. I had a new hideout in fashionable Drammensvei. It was a third-floor flat with no means of escape—not ideal—but suitable in other respects. The owner, Mrs. Berg, who lived there alone with her maid, must have realized there was some mystery about her new lodger, but she never asked questions. Then one day I found an envelope lying on the table in my room. In it was a large sum of money in notes for me to use "in the work you do."

My tactics were still the same: I never returned during the day to the place where I spent the night, but had my meals elsewhere. Then at last I learned to drive a car, and after that I drove all sorts of cars about Oslo. They all had false license plates and my driving license was one I had made myself. It was a very good one and I even got it renewed in 1945. I was always careful to park my cars a considerable distance away from my various dwellings. I also used a bicycle quite a lot, especially when meeting Hauge, the head of Milorg. We would meet at a pre-arranged crossing or in a square, and then bicycle together exchanging information and news as we rode. Hauge was one of the few who knew my hideout in Drammensvei and we also used to meet up at Skillebekk.

One of our great props at this time was a man called Pipe Lars. He was really Fritz Andresen. He was a friend of my former collaborator, Sverre Ellingsen, and also of Hans Halvorsen, whose special job was finance. He found the money for our work, and Pipe Lars had helped him for years, taking aid to many people and never getting involved himself. Help was often very necessary in homes where the husband or father had had to go into hiding or to Sweden, or had been arrested.

Morland and I now had a lot to do with Pipe Lars, who had endless friends and connections. Not only that, but he and his wife put their home at our disposal. They regarded the risk as a perfectly natural one to run.

That spring, by which time I was properly attached to the Central Committee, another two-man team from England was dropped near Oslo. They were to act as arms instructors and be available for special missions. I was soon in contact with these two, Andreas Aubert whom I already knew, and Henrik Hop, who came from Bergen. I acted as their liaison and had a lot to do with them. One of the first things, of course, was to find them somewhere to live. This I did through Mrs. Collett and Rev. Hauge, the Akershus Chaplain. The latter had a friend living in a large two-storied house with rooms to spare and we approached him. It was remarkable how we were never refused, even when we didn't come with introductions from such good friends as in this case. Homes were put at our disposal without question, even though the owners ran risks that became exceedingly grave as the German reprisals became harsher.

Strictly speaking, each little group from England was supposed to operate independently, but Oslo is not a big city and, when a group had to be in it for any length of time, they were pretty well bound to run into the other sooner or later; sometimes even in the street. Thus, though it was not part of our service, we found ourselves providing the men from England with explosives, food, transport, and special contacts.

By 1944 most of the NORIC people in Oslo knew of each other's presence there without having any fixed contact.

In Oslo itself, there were Max Manus and Gregers Gram from the group come to sabotage ships in the harbor; the recent arrivals, Andreas Aubert and Henrik Hop, who came under Milorg's Central Committee; and two instructors come to Oslo after successfully sabotaging the Smelting Works at Arendal. In addition, District 13 had two men from UK. Gradually, I became liaison officer among these different individuals and, to a certain extent, between them and the Central Committee. That, of course, wasn't good security, but it had worked before so why shouldn't I carry on with the contacts I had?

CHAPTER XIV

We Blow up the Labor Office

The winter of 1943-44 had not been a happy time for the Resistance Movement in Oslo. Many had been arrested and the clandestine press had almost been put out of action. It became obvious that our Nazis had plans for making more effective use of a Norwegian labor force. This led to repeated rumors during the winter of a labor draft. Now developments on the various fronts were making the Nazis desperate and they could be expected to do something drastic.

The leaders of our Home Front, who had the people under a certain degree of control, realized slogans and verbal encouragement would no longer be enough, and we began seriously planning more drastic action.

At the beginning of May, 1944, it was decided to institute a country-wide wave of sabotage. We would blow up the records of the Labor Service and so hinder or delay the labor draft. The idea originated with the civil organization of the Home Front, but it fell to Milorg to carry it out, effectively and successfully. Nonetheless, that month, what the leaders of the Home Front had so long feared came about: The puppet government agreed to help the Germans by mobilizing young Norwegians. It was called a Labor draft, but there was reason to fear that our young people might also be used as troops. Three different year-groups were to be called up. The matter was discussed with London and it was decided that we dare not risk letting this draft take place.

The mood of the country had improved after the wave of sabotage actions against the Labor Service. People had been aroused, but they were still not yet fully aware of the situation, and the leaders of the Home Front did not feel that mere exhortation to resist the labor draft would cause it to fail. They were convinced that stronger means would have to be used, so we began to discuss acts of sabotage that we might carry out to dramatize the strong resistance movement in the country and to instill more courage into the people. The country was to be made to know that any attempt to use young Norwegians as troops on the Eastern Front would be thwarted.

The first thing to be done, we decided, was to destroy Watson & Company's registering machines, which were to be used in preparing the draft cards for dispatch. This would cause the conscription to be delayed, and we hoped it would have a positive effect on the people.

The machines were on the ground floor of a building in Nedre Vollgate, and late one evening two of our men threw a couple of rocks through the window, jumped in, and began to fix charges with short fuses to the machines. The noise of the window breaking naturally attracted the attention of those who lived nearby, but the two had time to finish their work and get away.

It was incredible how quickly the news spread that the machines had been destroyed. At first, not everyone realized why they had been blown up, but this was soon explained in our secret newspapers.

Two of the Noric men in Oslo, Max Manus and Gregers Gram, who were both interested in the political side of things, were supposed to wage Psychological Warfare, which we cheerfully called propaganda. Gram had been trained for this in England and was especially interested in the subject. He was afraid that our Nazis would succeed with their draft, and both he and I were stout advocates of strong counter measures. In fact, we wanted to answer every move of the Nazis with as strong a counter-move as we could manage. Fortunately, the Home Front, encouraged by the success of the actions so far undertaken, had adopted the same view.

It was not strange that the mood of the people was close to resignation and apathy, a situation that could have developed into a national tragedy. To many people it seemed that the Resistance only caused additional misery, without really getting anywhere. It was a difficult time for the Milorg people, who could only exhort people to have patience. The war seemed to be dragging on and on. People had wearied of rumors that the Allies were going to set up a Second Front.

On the afternoon of May 18, the day before the young people had to register for the labor draft (which in Oslo they were to do at the Labor Office in Akers Street) I had a telephone call from Jens Hauge, asking me to meet him. We arrived at the appointed place, both on bicycles. Then we rode on together down Akers Street, and as we passed the Labor Office at No. 55, Hauge told me that something must be done with the place we were then passing. He asked me to see to it, explaining that I was the only person he could get hold of at the moment and the matter was urgent. I certainly had nothing against such a job, but they were not giving me much time in which to do it.

Hauge and his friends in the Home Front had concluded that it would be tremendously effective propaganda if the Labor Office at 55 Akers Street was blown up, so young people who turned up in the morning to register would find nothing but smoldering rubble.

It was then five o'clock in the afternoon, and it was also essential that the place be blown up while there was still daylight; in other words not later than eight o'clock. The sooner it could be done, the earlier the news would spread through the city and those due to register would hear of it.

I managed to find Gregers Gram and told him what was afoot. We decided to share the work involved: he was to get hold of Morland and go to our store in Kongens Street and prepare the charges of explosive, while I went back to Akers Street to reconnoiter No. 55 and get keys for it, if necessary. When Gram heard that the whole thing was to be done in a couple of hours, his jaw dropped, but he quickly got into the spirit of the thing.

Through a friend, I got in touch with a man high in the Labor Office. I told him that I wanted keys, but did not say why. He told me the office was full of people feverishly working to get everything ready for the next day's registering in the labor conscription. He thought there must be fifteen or twenty people working overtime at that very minute. But by six-thirty he had got me a key to the outer door. At seven o'clock I met Gregers Gram. Hanging on his handle bars he had a small black suitcase containing fifteen pounds of plastic explosive fitted with a two-minute fuse.

We had had no time to lay a proper plan, but quickly concluded that the only thing to do was to let ourselves in with the key, walk up, and lay the charges in a suitable place. Then, while Gram lit the fuse, I would go around the offices warning people that the building was going up in two minutes. We agreed that it was most important that no one should be hurt.

Just before he left our store, Gram had managed to get in touch with Max Manus, and we met him at the corner just before we turned in to Akers Street. He caught on in a trice and did not need to be asked if he would help. We were glad of the reinforcement.

We entered the courtyard at No. 55 and leaned our bicycles against the wall. Manus was to cover us, in case there was any trouble. We let ourselves in, went up to the second floor, and in through the door of the actual Labor Office. Gram went to a corner, put his little suitcase down, and got to work. I went across to the long wall with hatches in it where you stood and filled in your form. I was wearing a light-colored anarak and I now put on a pair of dark glasses. When Gram signalled that he was lighting the fuse, I shouted:

"Come on out of there! The building's being blown up. You've two minutes to get out."

Then I opened a door and shouted the same to some people in there. Fortunately everyone took the warning seriously. There was a bit of a crowd on the landing, but Gram said coldly: "We go first!" and we tore down the stairs with a tail of civil servants behind us.

Manus was relieved to see us, but he realized that with all those people around us we must get away quickly. We mounted our bicycles and pedalled up the street. We had not gone more than fifty yards when we heard a tremendous roar and saw bricks and glass and window-frames showering into the street behind us.

Farther down the street I dismounted, took off my anarak and sun glasses, and bicycled about for a while before going to the house where Morland was spending the evening. When Morland heard that we had done the trick, he was anxious to know what people were saying about it. We didn't think it a good idea to send any of the group down to 55 Akers Street, to which crowds were flocking, as the Germans had been known to arrest everybody who stopped to gape on such occasions; but we got hold of one of our contacts, Mrs. Dagmy Smith, and she volunteered to go down and see the damage and hear what people were saying. She came back and told us that the explosion seemed to have put everyone in a wonderful humor.

As both the papers and the offices were destroyed, the draft had to be postponed and that fact alone gave a great boost to people's morale. I was delighted to have done a job like that. At last I was doing what I had been wanting to do the whole time.

CHAPTER XV

Across the Roof-Tops

Not long after we blew up 55 Akers Street, we were asked to do a similar job for a similar purpose. We learned that our destruction of the Watson's machines had delayed, but was not going to prevent, the dispatch of the draft cards, because there was another machine in the city and this had been requisitioned for the job. The second machine was on the third floor of an insurance company's building, and I was asked to see that it was put out of action.

This was not as simple a business as the first. I made several reconnaissance trips and had to discuss the matter with a number of people before I could find out the location's weak points and the attack most likely to succeed.

The building was guarded by one guard in mufti at the ground floor entrance and four men on the third floor where the machine was. As far as we could ascertain, several of the guards belonged to the State Police.

I got hold of the rest of the group, and we made a plan to blow the machine up on Saturday evening, May 27. A member of the Night Watch Company had got me a key to the main door of the building, and we planned to go in and overpower the man in the downstairs passage; half of our number would remain below on guard, while the other three would go to the third floor to lay the charges in the machine.

The six of us were merely men in a Saturday evening crowd that filled the streets of Oslo. We walked about in pairs. Suddenly one pair turned aside and stopped at the entrance to a building. I was one of that pair.

I produced my key, opened the door, and in we went. I saw the guard in the passage, walked up to him and told him that I was a friend of "Mr. Gulberg in charge of the Labor Draft" and had a message for the men on the third floor. I asked if I could go up. The man thought this over and seemed almost on the point of accepting it. Then I said to him:

"Do you see the man there in the passage?"

Yes, he saw him all right. I went on:

"He has a pistol with a silencer aimed at you."

The pistol had rather a long barrel and my companion was holding it under his overcoat. He now let his overcoat fall open and the guard stared into the muzzle of a pistol. I relieved the man of his pistol, a little .25 that made me feel almost sorry for him, especially as he was just an ordinary policeman on extra duty, and not a member of the beastly State Police. We had a little talk with him, at the end of which we decided that it would be best for him if we gave him a tap on the head and knocked him out so he wouldn't get into trouble when the Germans appeared on the scene. My companion undertook to do this with his pistol. The first blow didn't do the trick, nor the second, but the third did and also made the darned pistol go off. Fortunately the bullet went over our heads.

Within a couple of minutes all six of us were safely inside. I and two of the others walked up the stairs. We had just passed the first floor when an alarm went off—at least we thought it was an alarm, though we never found out for sure—at all events we heard a great trampling and shuffling of feet on the second and third floors.

According to our information, we had no chance of carrying out our plan unless we could take the guards on the third floor unawares. This being so, I gave the signal to abandon the project and we hurried back down the stairs and out into the street, taking the others with us. Once outside, we scattered in all directions, furious at not having been able to do the job, which wasn't going to be any easier because of our unsuccessful attempt. When they found that the downstairs guard had been knocked out, they were pretty likely to strengthen the guard.

We made our second attempt the evening of Whit Monday. We now had a different plan, having discovered that we could approach the place via one of Andersen's shops. If we went through the back yard of the bakery building, we would find a backstairs to the third floor of the Insurance building, which we thus ought to reach unseen.

We arranged to meet at a cafe at half-past ten on Whit Monday. Because of unexpected delays I was late. The others sat waiting. After a while it struck them that there was something suspicious about some of the people who were walking to and fro in the vicinity. It became obvious that both the Germans and the State Police had people out looking for these awful saboteurs who had been so active in Oslo recently. My companions decided it was time to depart. They stood up and began to saunter away. All got away except Edvard Tallaksen. He was followed by a man in mufti, whom Tallaksen sensed to be a Gestapo creature. Tallaksen stopped and waited, hand on the revolver in his pocket. The man came right up to him, pulled out a pistol and hissed at him:

"Ausweis!"

Tallaksen's reply was to shoot from his pocket. The German dropped with a cry. Tallaksen tried to run, but whichever way he turned, he saw Germans coming at him. He had a very cool head and incredible luck. He managed to duck under the steps of a nearby house. There he stayed, holding in his hand a grenade he had been carrying in his pocket.

Tallaksen appeared next morning at his hideout, after rather a grim night. Because of what he had been through, we decided not to include him in our third attempt to destroy the machines. He protested, of course, but we pointed out that we needed only three men to carry out our new plan.

The guards on the machine and the building had been doubled but, after further reconnaissance and study, I had discovered a possible new approach. If we could get onto the roof of a house some distance away, we could make our way across the roofs to the building. This was flat with a door leading down. If we could get through this and down to the fourth floor and could lay a sufficiently strong charge on the floor and immediately above the machine, we could pulverize it.

In order to stick to our principle of not taking human lives unnecessarily, even those of Norwegian Nazis, we made a plan for warning the guards in time for them to get out.

The Night Watch company had again provided me with keys. There was no difficulty about getting into the arcade behind the building. From there, we got onto the roof of the first building easily. A little further down the street from the arcade, one of the group had a hideout on the fourth floor, and there we gathered in the afternoon. We had thirty pounds of explosive ready in a small suitcase. The spring nights were still light, so we had selected the darkest time for the attempt, which was between midnight and half-past twelve. Fortunately, the skies were overcast and there was a little rain, so conditions weren't bad.

The caretaker at the arcade let us in. We got to the attic of the house and put a ladder up to the trapdoor in the roof. One of the group was to remain there to cover us against surprises and to open the trapdoor when we returned. We had had no opportunity to rehearse our plan, and the arcade caretaker's description was all we had had to go by.

Experience had taught me that there were always surprises. I had come to expect the unexpected. What would it be this time? First, we scrambled over the roofs of several intervening houses. The roofs were steep and slippery from rain. The last house before our objective had Hotel Norrona lettered above the facade and was said to be inhabited by Germans. There was a stretch of flat roof with some windows looking onto it. These were open and we could hear German voices distinctly, but the curtains were closely drawn because of the blackout. Even so, there wasn't much between us and the Hotel Norrona's guests.

When we got to our objective, we found its roof was ten feet higher than that of the hotel. That meant we had to go back across the roofs and fetch the ladder we had used to get up onto the first one. It was a tricky business getting the ladder across the roofs, but we did it, and before long we were on the roof of the insurance building. It was no joke climbing that ladder onto the roof in full view of the street five floors below, clutching a suitcase with thirty pounds of explosive in it.

Up on the flat space on the roof, we fished out the key one of the people in the Insurance Company had got for us, and unlocked the door to the back stairs. We knew that the guards now had dogs with them, and we would have to be very cautious.

We stole down to the floor below and unlocked the door of the room immediately above the office in which the machine was. This actually was the canteen. We laid the suitcase with the explosive in the middle of the floor according to plan, and one of us pushed the pencil fuses in. That gave us seven to eight minutes. Then we stole back onto the roof and were careful to take the ladder with us. It would have been identifiable evidence that would have got the caretaker of the arcade into trouble, if we had left it.

Our guard at the trapdoor now jumped onto his bicycle, rode to the nearest telephone box, and called the guards at the Insurance building, telling them the place was going up in a couple of minutes. The guard consisted of five or six men. Fortunately for them, they took the warning seriously and were downstairs and out quickly. Shortly afterwards there was a roar as the charge went off. When again there was no loss of life, our sabotage had much more propaganda effect. It showed that the Resistance Movement was not to be stopped, yet it was humanitarian.

After telephoning to the guards our man had to get back to the flat where we had originally gathered—a risky business. We managed it. From our fourth-floor room we watched the activities of the Gestapo in the street below.

My driver had to get out of the country. One of his contacts had been arrested and we were afraid that he might not be able to stand up to interrogation. We decided that the driver ought to take his wife with him. This was easier said than done for it was no lark getting across to Sweden in April of 1944.

They were to use what was then one of the main routes for refugees. They were included in a batch of thirty-eight who piled onto two trucks which were to take them to Rödesnessjö, a long strip of water that runs parallel with the main road and the frontier between Kroksund and almost as far down as the main east road to Karlstad into Sweden. There the refugees were to walk across the ice and over the boundary. Their guides were the two truck drivers. One of them was making his last trip to the frontier, after which he was going to become my new driver in Oslo.

When they reached the lake, they were unable to take the usual way across because the ice was beginning to break. When they were well within the frontier zone, they ran smack into a couple of guards armed with machine guns. The two guides opened fire. There was a violent exchange of shots and one of the guides was killed. So were the two frontier guards. All the refugees got across the frontier without further incident.

Thoresen, who had driven his own truck, saw only one way out—to escape to Sweden himself.

CHAPTER XVI

Hunted but Cheerful

Our little group had now acquired a small fleet of cars, which we drove about using false license plates with numbers given us by friends in the Traffic Department. Two brothers who had a garage and a very reliable staff of mechanics serviced them for us. They attached the false plates, resprayed a car when it became advisable to change its appearance, and did our repairs.

I often noticed the mechanics grinning when they took a look at the connections between our generators and the engines. And well they might, because we always drove on gasoline, thanks to our friends in two of the big oil companies in Norway. Immediately after the occupation each of them had secreted 50,000 gallons of gasoline which they handed over to us, giving us fuel for a long time. We also had a big van which always had a permit displayed on its windscreen from the State Grain Commission or the Department of Roads and Highways. We had a truck which was really an old car adapted to its new purpose. It had a powerful Nash motor, and a carbide-generator fixed on at the back for show. Morland usually drove the van and I the Nash. We also had the Opel Olympia that my second driver had driven. Then we had a 1938 Chevrolet which had a gas generator which was not only properly connected, but on which it could run as well as on gasoline. Later, I had the use of a Mercedes 170, which also had a carbide generator and something resembling a connection with the engine. There was not much traffic in Oslo, and it was rather fun tearing through the streets on dark evenings. When a car came along with blackout covers over its headlamps no one could tell whether it was German or Norwegian. There were plenty of controls and check-points now; in fact they were such everyday occurrences that we had ceased to mention them.

One day I ran into one of these check-points at Majorstua while driving the truck. On the bridge behind me I had a Sten machine gun bundled up in newspaper. That was not as foolhardy as it sounds because, when dismantled, a Sten gun looks like a lot of plumber's scrap, all very innocent and lawful. The Germans looked at the bundle, but it never occurred to them that it might have anything to do with underground activities.

We had good friends in the Highway Department and they provided us with all sorts of passes and permits. We had another great asset in a workshop of the ESSO Company's transport department. There we could be sure of getting help day or night.

Another vehicle at our disposal was a big blue truck used by the Danish Help organization, for which my original ESSO contact was now working as a full-time driver. We were careful not to use this truck for any job which could compromise the Danish Help organization. This organization had access to the prisons and on occasion I went with it as "driver's mate" into the prison at Akerbergvei. It was an eerie feeling when the gate closed behind us.

One day, however, we nearly did compromise the blue truck. we had used it to take some supplies to Haugland at the Gynecological Clinic, where he was still living and where he worked his transmitter. We had just turned onto the street that led to the main gate, when we found that we had motor bicycles on either side of us, and were in the middle of a group of armed police. There must have been a full company of them. All we could do was drive on. We couldn't speed nor, of course, did we stop at the gate to the Gynecological Clinic. I was standing behind the driver's cab and had a good view of everything. The suspense was unnerving. Would we be stopped? Would our papers be accepted? Would they search us?

We weren't stopped. Instead the Germans motioned to us to get a move on. We were just in the way as far as they were concerned. We drove past the Clinic and sped away.

Some hours later I was in touch with Knut Haugland and learned what had happened. A hundred Germans had been sent to take him. The whole Clinic was ringed, but he shot his way out and managed to get clear. We found him another hideout and he had to lie low for a while. There had already been talk of his going back to England, and he could not stay on in Oslo after this. We waited a few days till the Germans had calmed down a bit, and then I was to see Haugland across to Stockholm.

For Haugland we broke our rules a second time and used the post route over Kongsvinger. At six o'clock in the morning of April 12, we mounted our bicyles and rode off. All day—and a bitterly cold day it was—we pedalled wearily through slush, reaching Kongsvinger late in the afternoon. We stopped at Engebretsen's garage and conferred with him. Engebretsen thought that we would have a clear road as far as our farm near Austmarka, and even beyond; but he told us to be especially careful when passing Austmarka itself, because there were some Norwegian frontier guards there now. These frontier guards were all picked men and Nazis. They of course knew almost all of the local inhabitants by sight and we, being strangers, might easily arouse their suspicions. Our papers were first-class fakes but still it would look suspicious for anyone to be at the frontier. In the circumstances, we decided that if our luck failed we must shoot it out and take the chance of getting into the forest and away. Unless the frontier guards we encountered were actually Norwegians, we felt pretty sure of getting away with it, for we were both pretty good at imitating lumbermen—certainly good enough to fool the Gestapo.

It was with more than a little excitement that we looked up towards the house on the hill, where the frontier guards were quartered, as we free-wheeled down into Austmarka. Then came the turn to the right; we were around and in the clear; and we headed for the farm and the lake, Utgaardsjoen. We were thoroughly exhausted and breathing heavily when we reached the farm. Here we rested for a bit.

Our relations with the Swedes were such that we could expect to be welcomed with open arms. At Tomta, our last farm on the Norwegian side, we listened to the London news bulletin and then walked across into Sweden and straight to the local customs man, Engelbrektsson. He served us a good meal and then telephoned the local deputy-sheriff, who came and got us in his car. We gave him the latest military information and went to bed. The next evening we were on the train heading for Stockholm.

Things had changed in Stockholm. Our office that had been directly under SOE's Swedish office now worked closely with the Norwegian Military Office. Here I came in contact with the Americans, who now had a branch of their OSS in Stockholm. I promised to keep a protective eye on their people in Oslo and get some of our people in touch with them.

I was not long in Stockholm on that occasion. After a few days I headed west again, crossed the frontier, and returned to Oslo. Our spirits were high now; sometimes we were even a bit too arrogant and too inclined to be funny at the Germans' expense, but certainly no one ever suspected that the gaily smiling young men who bicycled about in the mid-morning, four or five in a cluster, were up to anything but horseplay and wasting their employers' time—least of all that they were Resistance agents who had been specially trained in England and parachuted into Norway.

One day, Morland, Gram and I had an errand at the Andersens' bakery, and we decided to go by tram. We stood on the back platform with a number of ordinary passengers. Gram was wearing glasses—with ordinary plain glass in them. We were laughing and playing the fools, and Morland told Gram he ought to take his glasses off because they looked as though they had plain glass in them. People began to stare at us, and we laughed so much we had to get off long before we meant to.

Often when I was with Gregers Gram, I would think: I do hope you come through. He was such a fine specimen of the best type of young Norwegian—tall, high forehead, and a mop of fair hair, he was gifted and full of spirit and humor. He always saw events in a broader perspective than we did. His main interest was in studying the psychology of the Germans. At the same time, he took a great interest in social problems. His head was always stuffed with plans, including what he was going to do when the war was over. He had been a student in Oslo, and it was incredible that he could go about the city as unconcernedly as he did.

One day a number of us were in a park. Three or four of us lounged on a seat; the others leaned on their bicycles. Then a grounds-keeper came up. I had been careless and ridden over his beautiful grass and the man had seen me do it. Rather peevishly he asked me how I could do such a thing. My answer must have been curt, perhaps even rude; for he lost his temper and we had quite a wordy exchange. In the end he demanded my name and wanted to see my identity card. I happened to have two identity cards on me that day—with the same photograph but different names, and the temptation was too much. I produced them both and told the man he could toss up which name to choose. The others roared with laughter, but the man was furious and bewildered. One look at the others, however, convinced him that he had better leave well alone and not pursue the matter. For a long time after that my comrades teased me with threats, not of the Gestapo, but of Sepapo, the Secret Park Police.

A few days later I had to show my identity card again, with more serious results. I was in our Opel driving along the road west of Oslo. I came to some crossroads at a place called Sandvika and two policemen, one in uniform, the other in mufti, signaled to me to stop. My first thought was that they must be the State Police, but I stopped. The men looked into the back of the car and then asked to see my identity card. I handed it to the one in mufti. On this card my name was Knut Sekkelsten, and it stated that I was employed by the Gas Generator Company and was born at a place called Eidsberg. The man's face lit up as he looked at my card, and I wondered what was coming. Then he said:

"But, Sekkelsten, I must know you."

"There are plenty of people called Sekkelsten," I replied.

"Yes, but my Sekkelstens come from Eidsberg."

"Very likely," I said. "There's another family of Sekkelstens. They have a farm not far from the one my father comes from."

But the man insisted.

"Yes, but the man I know was born in the same year as you."

"Well, I can't help that."

In the end, the man became really irritated and muttered something to the uniformed policeman beside him. The man in mufti then announced that he was going to call up the Gas Generator Company to check up on me. In the meantime I was to drive to the side of the road.

For a moment I hesitated, I had a Colt .45 in the pocket of the car door and my first thought was to use it and drive off. Fortunately, I didn't. I acted as though I were going to draw to the road side, jammed my foot on the accelerator, and drove off in the direction of Oslo.

What I didn't realize at the time was the two were looking for vegetables being smuggled in to Oslo, and the one in mufti was a man from the Price Control Board. That made the whole thing rather ridiculous, but it had a serious side, because the incident was reported to the Germans. They concluded I must be one of the men they were looking for and set up road blocks into the city. However, I was an old hand by now and, when I reached the suburbs, I drove up a side street, parked the car, and a few minutes later was sitting in the suburban railway. I got out at the central terminal.

I was irritated at having had to leave the car and also at having compromised it. We dared not risk using it again. I had unscrewed the false license plates and chucked them into the luggage compartment before I left it. Still, I had to dispose of it so I took the first train out in the morning to the place where I had left the car. Leaving the license plates where they were, I drove straight to Haslum and into a manure-cellar. There the car stood, over its axles in liquid manure, for several months. It was far from a fragrant object when we eventually retrieved it.

This incident led to further teasing. They now threatened me with the "Vegstapo."

I was fortunate not to have used my pistol at Sandvika, if only because the two men were decent fellows. The one in mufti was quite right about his Knut Sekkelsten. There was one in the Gas Generator Company. Our contact man there had provided correct details for my card, so it was a copy of a genuine one. That I should have been stopped by someone who knew the real Sekkelsten was a piece of circumstantial bad luck.

The policeman at Sandvika had called the Gas Generator Company and spoken with the true Knut Sekkelsten. He immediately informed our contact man, who passed the news on to others of the group. They thought I had been arrested, and drove out to Sandvika. There they met the man in mufti and learned that I had driven off while he was calling the Gas Generator Company. He was a decent fellow and agreed to hand over my papers, which he still had. That ended his career as a policeman, so he went back to Oslo with them. They promised to send him across to Sweden at once. He wasn't even to take the risk of going back to his office.

We had contacts in the State Police and they were of tremendous help to us. These were men in the resistance movement, who went on working for it while in the State Police—a difficult and hazardous thing to do. Apart from this risk, these men's families had to suffer social disapproval because people knew where their husbands and fathers were employed and naturally assumed they were Nazis.

Then our main contact in the State Police, a man called Lovstuhagen, was arrested and horribly tortured. He magnificently avoided giving away any secrets or naming his collaborators. Later he was sent to Germany. He was one of the lucky few who came back. His arrest interrupted our flow of information for a while, but after a bit Lovstuhagen's wife introduced another member of the Stapo group to Morland and this fruitful contact was resumed.

Through these men we had comprehensive knowledge of what the enemy were up to. The Germans did not use the Norwegian State Police for the most important assignments but we were able to find out about many people whom the Germans arrested. Often our informants could tell us which department was dealing with a case and from that we knew pretty well what the charge was. Ultimately these men got so well acquainted with our affairs that they could tell whether we were likely to be involved in any arrests the Germans were planning, and after our coups could tell us what eyewitnesses had said and whether there was any dangerous evidence.

It was, in fact, largely due to our friends in the State Police that seven or eight men from England were able to live and work in Oslo as they did. Their most valuable help was the warnings they gave us. They tipped us off about forthcoming arrests, and ran great risks in doing so; when any such leak occurred, suspicion could only fall on a limited number. In time, these warnings were organized and we received them through the Central Committee.

In the spring of 1944 Per Morland was seen in the street by one of the few Norwegians who collaborated with the Germans—a man who knew that he had gone to Sweden long before. Morland was unaware that he had been seen, but fortunately one of our contacts in the

State Police saw the report and noticed Morland's name. The State Police should have sent the report on to the German Sicherheitspolizei, but somehow it never got there.

Morland, I and seven or eight of the men from England had equipped ourselves with State Police identity cards and badges provided by our friends there. I had told the others that they were to be used only in extreme emergencies and that they must leave them at home if they were setting out on a dangerous mission. When on such business, they probably would have to use weapons if they ran into a roadblock, so identity cards didn't much matter.

I used my State Police pass frequently and was always surprised at how easy it was to get through all check points. Of course, it was buttressed by the fact that I was driving a car with one of the State Police's secret numbers. When posing as a member of the State Police, I usually drove our Chevrolet. If I had ever been stopped by the State Police themselves, I would have had little chance, because they all knew each other, but with the Germans and others it was easy. Naturally, there was always a moment or two of excitement, but it was a glorious feeling knowing how beautifully I was taking them in.

CHAPTER XVII

More Sabotage

In the middle of June I was told to break into an office belonging to the Akershus Branch of the Rationing Authority. This office was in Oslo's main street, Karl Johan. As usual I went to my friend in the Night Watch Company and he got me a key to the main door. That was excellent, but there were other doors that my companion and I would have to open. In England I had had a lesson or two in the gentle art of housebreaking and had had a little practice at the end of 1942 when a group arrived from England which included a famous Norwegian safecracker (now a respectable and respected member of society), who trained the whole group and taught us all a lot about opening locks. For this instruction we needed a certain amount of equipment and one of the group had to go to an ironmonger's and buy it. He went to a shop where he knew one of the assistants. When the man had looked through the list of wire and tools that he was being asked to supply, he said:

"If I didn't know you so well, I'd ring up the police, because this is housebreaking equipment pure and simple."

So it was, and thanks to it, I was quite adept at opening locked doors.

We let ourselves into the Rationing Authority's office, and the rest went as planned. I had the Yale lock open in a jiffy and we walked in and took the ration cards we had been told to get.

During June I was put in touch with a small group which was to assist me in planning industrial sabotage. I first met the group in a little flat on Oscars Street. I walked up to it, was admitted, and was told to put on a mask. I was then ushered into a room where sat three men whose faces were completely covered by black masks. From our conversation it was obvious that the three were familiar with Norwegian industry. We discussed a plan to knock out the explosives factories. The manufacturers themselves had suggested the plan, apparently. The idea was to paralyze the factories by cutting off the supply of sulphuric acid on which they depended. There were two factories manufacturing concentrated sulphuric acid for the explosives industry—one at Lysaker and one at Hurum—and the idea was to blow up the retorts and storage tanks. Civilian requirements of sulphuric acid could be met by other means.

The plan was adopted and I was sent to various people in the Oslo headquarters of the chemical industry who gave me all the technical data and information I needed.

The explosives industry was an important part of German war production in Norway—explosives being necessary for the construction of fortifications, naval bases, etc. To attack these factories directly would have caused great difficulty and inconvenience to civilian consumers, apart from the fact that it could easily lead to a catastrophe. The stoppage of the supply of sulphuric acid, on the other hand, would reduce output enough to sabotage war production.

Having obtained my technical data and information, I met with my trained men from England. We had to reconnoiter the two factories to find out about guards, patrols, the exact sites of our objectives, how to get in through gates and fences, and things like that. We decided it would be best to carry out both jobs on the same day; otherwise, the Germans and State Police would be bound to increase the guard and strengthen their security measures at the remaining factory.

Birger Rasmussen and I were to deal with the factory at Lysaker; and four of the others were assigned the one at Hurum. Reconnoitering the factory at Lysaker was easy. We had a contact there and he drew a sketch map for us. One or two visits showed there was no German guard on the place, though there were German troops at a nearby school and at Lysaker. Reconnaissance at Hurum was not so easy, but the local Milorg people helped get all the necessary information.

The two jobs were to be attempted on June 28. It was a lovely evening and as light as day. Rasmussen and I had put on overalls and were carrying heavy bags looking (we hoped) like a couple of plumbers working overtime. We had no difficulty in getting to the factory area, which we did through a hole in the fence. There were no guards or sentries to be seen.

We made straight for the two acid tanks and fixed an appropriate charge to each, fitted with a "pencil" time fuse. This is a tube, like a pencil, containing a glass cylinder filled with acid. Pressure on a knob breaks the glass, spilling the acid, which then attacks a thin copper wire. When this is eaten through, it releases a hammer which strikes the detonator and sets it off, igniting the charge. This done, we went into the factory and fixed charges to the two acid-retorts. For these we used quite small charges, having promised the owners of the factory not to destroy any of the rest of the plant. The charges were fixed where we could camouflage them and feel reasonably sure that they would not be discovered. The time fuse was set for ten minutes. The charges were to be exploded simultaneously with those at Verpen, thirty five miles to the west.

By this time, the Germans knew English-trained were at work in the Oslo area; to avoid reprisals on the civilian population, we arranged to take some pieces of British uniform and equipment with us and drop these near the scenes of sabotage, hoping the Germans would think the operations had been carried out by troops parachuted into the area. The trick worked. Our friends in the State Police told us that it had been a scene of triumph when the Germans found the things.

Having set off the fuses, we quietly bicycled back to Oslo. The experts said later we had done our work very successfully. Both retorts were destroyed: no other equipment was damaged. The other four saboteurs were equally successful at Hurum.

On Saturday July 8, I learned to my dismay that my good contact John Myhre had been arrested and was in the hands of the Gestapo. I quickly sent word to Stockholm to warn contacts there that they must not come back to Oslo for the time being. Fortunately, I was able to let them know a few days later that all was well. Myhre had been released. He had undergone a grilling, but had miraculously

Claus Helberg during the occupation, as a secret wireless operator
in the Rjukan mountains.

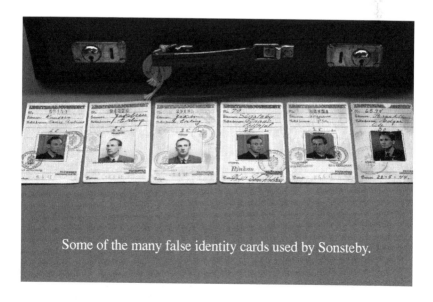

Some of the many false identity cards used by Sonsteby.

Per Morland was Sønsteby's nearest companion. To solve difficult assignments they used false identities and police uniforms.

The Resistance Leader Knut Moyen.

The suitcase. A selection of Sonsteby's working tools in his everyday function as SOE operative. False identities, police evidence and access cards, etc.

The labor office, destroyed.

Tor Greiner Stenersen.
Member of oslogjengen.
Killed by Germans during
an escape attempt from
Akershus Fortress.

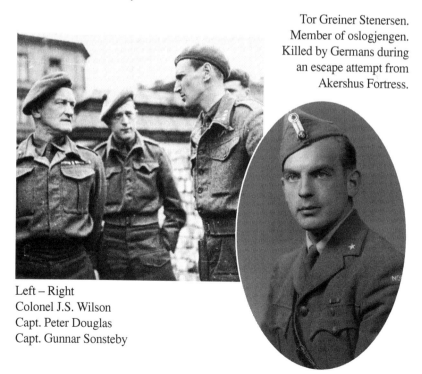

Left – Right
Colonel J.S. Wilson
Capt. Peter Douglas
Capt. Gunnar Sonsteby

Top secret visit from High Command in London. Colonal Oen second from the right.

Johan Edvard Tallaksen.
He was seriously wounded in a gunfight with the Gestapo and arrested.
To avoid spoiling his comrades, he chose to take his own life in prison.

Lieutenant Knut Haugland and Capt. Ragnar I. Christophersen.

UNITED STATES SPECIAL OPERATIONS COMMAND

TO ALL WHO SHALL SEE THESE PRESENTS, GREETING:
THIS IS TO CERTIFY THAT
THE COMMANDER HAS AUTHORIZED THE AWARD OF THE

UNITED STATES SPECIAL OPERATIONS COMMAND MEDAL

TO

Kaptein Gunnar Sønsteby
Norwegian Army

FOR
OUTSTANDING CONTRIBUTIONS
TO SPECIAL OPERATIONS

GIVEN UNDER MY HAND AT MACDILL AIR FORCE BASE, TAMPA, FLORIDA
THIS 18th DAY OF June 2008

ERIC T. OLSON
Admiral, U.S. Navy
Commander

Sønsteby was awarded the United States Special Operations Command Medal in 2009. The medal was presented by chief of special forces, Admiral Eric Olson.

The United States Special Operations Command Medal.

CITATION

TO ACCOMPANY THE AWARD OF

THE UNITED STATES SPECIAL OPERATIONS COMMAND MEDAL

TO

KAPTEIN GUNNAR SØNSTEBY
NORWEGIAN ARMY

Kaptein Gunnar Sønsteby, Norwegian Army, distinguished himself through exemplary heroism during the Second World War while serving as a Norwegian Resistance Fighter in numerous assignments and missions during the period 1940 through 1945. Known also as Kjakan "The Chin" and "No. 24", Kaptein Sønsteby was a master of disguise and remained untouchable through the use of nearly 40 fictitious identities. His resistance efforts included working for an underground newspaper; travelling as a courier between Oslo, Norway and Stockholm, Sweden; serving as the British special operations executive-resident in Oslo establishing a network of safe houses and conduits; being the mastermind behind the smuggling of Norwegian currency dies to Stockholm, Sweden for the printing of banknotes. His numerous courageous actions climaxed with a series of daring sabotage actions against important military, industrial, railroad, aviation, as well as oil and fuel targets. Kaptein Sønsteby's daring actions contributed to the weakening of the enemy and to setting the conditions for liberation of Norway. His superior abilities, broad military experience, and dynamic leadership have raised the standards and inspired future generations of special operations warriors while reflecting great credit upon him, the Norwegian military, and Special Operations Forces worldwide.

Citation US SOCOM Medal.

Germans try to rescue
some of the planes after
the sabotage at Bjolsen.

Jens Christian Hauge,
the resistance leader.

Gregers Gram, resting in
neutral Sweden, 1944

Inside the machine hall.

William Houlder
and Max Manus.

Tramway Hall at
Bjolsen in Oslo.
This was the
Germans' main
yard for plain
repairs. The
workshop was
blown up by
oslogjengen and
large amounts of
aircraft engines
and fighter planes
were destroyed.

Gunnar Sonsteby's unique collection of medals. As the only one, he is awarded Norway's highest award, War Cross with Sword, three times!

Citation US Medal of Freedom with Silver Palm.

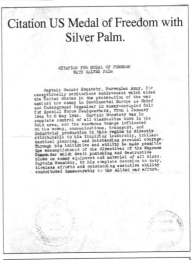

In 2001 Sonsteby was awarded The American - Scandinavian Foundation Cultural Award. The prize is awarded to individuals who " ... *by their efforts have contributed significantly to a better understanding between the United States and the Scandinavian countries.*"

A letter of Introduction. Major General William J. Donovan was the commander of the special department OSS during the war. After the war he was involved in the creation of the CIA. Sonsteby and Donovan were good friends after the war.

persuaded the Gestapo people that he would work for them if they let him go! They had released him and he had immediately gone into hiding. We were soon in touch with him. At that time several of our refugee routes were no longer usable, so it wasn't easy getting Myhre out of the country. We arranged to send him by boat from Sandefjord across to the coast of Sweden. On July 11, I drove up in one of our cars, Myhre and a cousin of his got in beside me, and I drove them to Sandefjord, where I handed them over to our contacts. A few days later they were in Sweden.

CHAPTER XVIII

We Capture a Load of Ration Cards

Quisling and his fellow Nazis did not do so well with their plan to call up the 1921-22-23 classes. They no doubt had visions of a whole Norwegian army that they could send to the Eastern Front to fight for Germany. The Germans wanted to mobilize the young Norwegians, too; but they had encountered unexpected resistance and were well aware that a Norwegian force of young people conscripted against their will would scarcely be reliable.

The urgent appeals issued by the Home Front to young people to refuse to allow themselves to be registered—appeals broadcast from London by radio, reproduced in the illegal press, and supported by sabotage operations—had produced results. Young people tried to avoid the draft in every possible way: They went into hiding with friends and acquaintances, went to huts, and disappeared into the mountains. Many of those who had already joined Milorg made their way to assembly points in the forests and agricultural districts. This deluge of resisters was a mixed blessing for Milorg, which had been given no time to organize an underground army outside the towns. There were no supplies, no accommodations and very few arms. Notice was given that only young people could be accepted who had special qualifications and athletic training.

Where would the food come from for all those people? There were thousands upon thousands of them hiding up and down the country.

The first crisis was hurdled by the joint efforts of all underground organizations, but the situation could only get worse and worse because, if a person was not found at home when the police went to fetch him, his ration card was canceled; and without ration cards the problem of feeding such a multitude was well-nigh insoluble.

Then it occurred to some clever people to intercept a shipment of ration cards when the printers sent a truck load to the post office. These people had a contact in the printing firm who could tell them when a consignment was being shipped. A truck load would be about 150,000 cards.

At this stage I was approached to help and advise. We sat on a seat in a square and discussed it all. The others asked me if it would be possible to stage a hold-up and then drive the truck to some place where its load could be transferred to another vehicle or vehicles. To me it sounded easy. We made our plans.

On August 9, I got up at seven o'clock, shaved, and ate a larger breakfast than usual. Then I got out my bicycle and rode down to Hausmannsbrua, which I reached a minute or two after eight. At 8:15 I met the two who were to do the job with me. A little way down the street stood a grey Ford with a gas-generator fixed on behind (and plenty of gas in the tank). In it sat three others.

The truck was to leave the printing works at about 8:30.

It came out of the gate of the printing plant a little earlier than expected. One of us signalled to the driver of the Ford, who drove up towards the crossing. The truck stopped to let the car from the right (which had the right of way) pass. I went up, opened the door of the driver's cab, and mounted the step. I had a pistol in my hand and, pointing it at the two men in the cab, told them to squeeze up and make room for me. As quietly and calmly as I could, I said:

"You must do as I say. We have two men who are getting up behind now. They are armed too and will shoot if necessary."

Everything went perfectly. When I was sure our two men were aboard, I told the driver to drive on towards the Post Office. The Ford followed forty or fifty yards behind. The three in it were armed with machine guns. It was a much bigger force than we really needed but conditions had been worsened by our recent acts of sabotage, and we were afraid the Nazis might have put extra guards on the ration cards at the last moment.

As we drove along, the men beside me calmed down. As we approached the Post Office, I told them we intended to take the load of ration cards. They wondered what on earth we could do with a ton of ration cards.

"That's our affair," I said. "But we'll find some use for them."

I also tried to persuade them that we weren't ordinary gangsters, but, judging by their expressions, I don't think I succeeded.

At the Post Office I told the driver to drive on to Tollbu Street and then to Skipper Street, where I told him to stop. I looked about for the group that was to take over the cards. I didn't know them by sight, but I had a pass-word and our contact man was to be standing outside No. 17.

Some minutes later we were in touch with the receiving party, whose car drove up behind the truck. I made the four printers' men turn their heads, and we put a box in front of the license plate to hide it. It took about ten minutes to transfer the load, during which time some of the others urged the men from the printers to go to Sweden because they might be suspected of complicity. Two agreed to go and, when the transfer of the cards had been completed, they jumped into our car and off we all went, but the other two decided not to go. It was now nearly nine o'clock, and the street was swarming with people hurrying to work. No one seemed to realize that a ton of ration cards was being stolen in front of his eyes.

We drove off towards Etterstad. On the way, one of the printers' men who was going to Sweden (whom we had not realized was in the Resistance) said that he had some incriminating stuff in his flat, and he thought he had better get rid of it. He surmised that the State Police would search his flat when the theft and his disappearance were discovered. We stopped the van and transferred into the Ford, which then drove to the man's home. I went up with him and helped him remove everything incriminating.

Then we caught up with the truck and drove on. Further on we thought we saw a German control-point ahead and turned into a side street. We tied the two who were not going to Sweden to the truck—as bystanders watched, who felt they must be seeing things! —so that they could plead *force majeur*, and the rest of us drove off.

Later, I could resist it no longer, but went to a telephone booth and rang up the printing works. When I got through, I asked to speak to the policeman on duty guarding ration cards. A very stern voice said: "Hallo."

"My name's Hansen," I said. "I'm sorry to have to tell you that we had to hold up the truck with the ration cards on its way to the Post Office."

At first, the man thought I was pulling his leg, but then he realized that I wasn't and began asking me eagerly to repeat my name and tell him where he could get hold of me.

"I don't think I want to do that," I replied and hung up.

Of course, it was a foolhardy gesture. I had not stopped to think that two of the printers' men were going to be sent to Sweden and they would want to go and get things. But fortunately all ended well.

With the vast quantity of ration cards in its possession, the Home Front had a valuable weapon. Cards in such numbers constituted a threat to the whole supply apparatus—as the Quisling Government was well aware—and chaos in the field of supply might easily irritate the Germans. Using devious channels so neither the Germans or Norwegian police could trace the communication to its source, we informed Quisling's Supply Minister that the cards would not be misused, would even be returned, if the order was rescinded that no ration cards should be issued to those evading registration for the labor draft.

The Quisling government capitulated utterly. We made our coup on Wednesday, August 9. The following Friday all Rationing Offices up and down the country received instructions to issue everyone ration cards without exception. Having won that round, the Home Front returned the cards: 70,000 ration books, 30,000 supplementary cards, and nearly 30,000 tobacco cards. Politically it was a fiasco for Quisling and his friends, and a few days later they tried to save face. The Norwegian press, which was under strict control, was sent a news item which all papers were ordered to print on the front page on Monday, August 14.

"Large quantity of Ration Cards stolen in transit
Criminals belong to an illegal organization"

The report went on to say that a reward of 200,000 Crowns was offered for information leading to the arrest of the thieves. But the really important part was the news that, as punishment for the theft, the whole population was to be deprived of five days' tobacco and alcohol rations. The Nazis thought this a great triumph. Now the people would vent their displeasure on the Resistance Movement. I must admit that this announcement was received with mixed feelings, but as soon as our clandestine press gave people the true story, there was much satisfaction with what we had done.

While we were planning our robbery of the ration cards, Mrs. Andersen warned me that my mother had been to see her at Gronland Street, because she was worried about me. My letters from Stockholm had almost convinced my mother that I was outside the country beyond reach of the Gestapo, but recently she had heard unsettling news. Apparently Mrs. Anderson finally managed to convince mother that I was in Sweden.

What had aroused mother's doubts was rather a strange story. Mother had some friends who lived at Grorud who had friends whose daughter had married one of the heads of the Labor Service. He was rather a questionable person, for he included the head of the Gestapo, SS-Sturmbannführer Reinhardt, in his private circle of acquaintances. Down this chain had come the information that Reinhardt was supposed to have said he knew that Gunnar Sonsteby was in the country.

This information was useful to me and I duly noted it.

The day after the ration-card hold-up I went to see Mrs. Andersen and her daughter. They suspected that we had done it, and it amused them both intensely. Then Mrs. Andersen told me she was expecting my mother that afternoon, and I ought not to stay long.

But it was already too late. The house telephone rang and a voice from the shop on the ground floor said Mrs. Sonsteby was on her way up. I could only dash into the office and wait. So, there I sat with my mother in the next room, unable to see her or tell her I was there. If she had learned I was in Oslo, it would have imposed a great nervous strain and it could have endangered her safety. It was enough that I had involved my father, I felt; I must try to avoid sending the whole family to prison!

I heard that all was well at Rjukan, and that the three radios she had taken there for me were being put to good use with friends, so she had no difficulty in hearing decent news and how the war was going. The situation was especially exciting now after the invasion of France.

While eavesdropping, I also heard that mother was in contact of a sort with father. It had been difficult to get to see him at Grini Prison.

but now he had been put in a so-called "Outside Kommando" and every day was taken by truck from Grini to the school at Majorstua where they made various things for the Germans. They were strictly guarded, but the guards were mostly ordinary German soldiers and they permitted a certain contact with the outer world. I think it was through the porter at the school that mother got her chance to talk with father and give him food parcels.

The Grini road was one I often had to drive and I was full of rage when I found myself behind one of those trucks with Grini prisoners. I stayed on the lookout for father but I never saw him. The sight of those trucks reinforced my determination to get at the Gestapo.

CHAPTER XIX

Two Big Bangs

Some time in July, Max Manus suggested a sabotage job to me. One of his assistants had discovered that the Germans had a large store of airplane parts in the garage of the Oslo Tramways at Korsvoll. This was a vast building, half of which the Germans had requisitioned. According to our informant, there were twenty-five Messerschmidt fighters and 150 airplane motors stored there, which must have made it the largest store of fighter parts in Norway.

I agreed with Manus that this was an attractive objective and we ought to have a try at it. Our superiors were interested, and London was asked its opinion. Manus and Gram had general permission from London to take part in the NORIC people's actions in and around Oslo, but London wanted to be informed in advance and to approve the objective. This latter stipulation applied to us all. I took the matter up with Milorg, which approved wholeheartedly.

Some days later we had a reply from London: Go ahead! Max Manus and a companion made a further study of the layout, and one day we were able to draft a plan. It was exhilarating for me and the three others of my group to be in on this operation.

Perhaps we weren't as clever as we thought, for we made two unsuccessful attempts. Having had plenty of warning, the Germans strengthened the guard inside the building. As a rule this guard was a mixture of Germans and Norwegians, the latter from a special guard battalion the Nazis had formed.

We made our third attempt during the night of August 13. Max Manus was in command. We assembled at 1:15 A.M. in a side street some 250 yards from the building. Then we walked straight to the Norwegian side of the building towards the entrance door. A companion and I continued right up to the door and picked the lock. Cautiously we went inside and took up a position in front of the next door so as to surprise the night watchman. He was a Norwegian. It was essential that he be rendered harmless without alarming the Germans on the other side of the building.

Being the most innocuous-looking of us all, I was to deal with the night watchman when he appeared, and I managed this without startling him or making him give the alarm. One of our men stayed behind to look after him, and the other five quietly went in. There is usually some unanticipated obstacle, and it was so in this case. When we entered the Norwegian part of the great hangar which was crammed with buses, we saw a gang of women cleaning them. They looked up in some surprise at their nocturnal visitors, but kept on with what they were doing. We did not look all that angelic, and I wondered how they would react when we went past them humping three hundred pounds of explosive, so while the others went down to the cellars to reconnoiter, I went across to engage the charwomen in conversation.

We had to cut through a triple-wire fence that barricaded the German side. Two of us attended to this, one guarded the corridor, and Manus himself watched the outer door. It took a good fifteen minutes to cut through the fence, and all the while I chatted with my charwomen. I told them that I was a poster-painter and sign-writer and was to paint a number of posters in the buses that night. I said the others were all tram-way men, but dabbled on the black market, and had a store of food in the cellars. The women swallowed it all and never turned a hair, even when Manus drove our car up to the door and we carried in the explosives, both plastic and ordinary dynamite, which were packed in three or four suitcases.

All was ready and the fuses were lit by two o'clock. The others came up and walked out, and I went across to the charwomen and warned them that the building would blow up in five minutes. They looked bewildered but eventually realized that I was in dead earnest and scrambled out. One of our men drove up in the car, Manus and his three jumped in and drove off, while my companion mounted his bicycle and pedaled away into the darkness.

All was done and ready: The night watchman had been freed, the charwomen were all out, and I could go too. The Germans had by now obviously got a hint that something was up, for we heard shouts of "Halt!" I jumped onto my bike and rode a couple of blocks. Then I stopped to wait for the explosion. I had hardly dismounted when I heard a tremendous roar which shook the ground under my feet. The task was done! I rode peacefully back to Vinderen where I had secured a couple of new hideouts.

Some months before this, in June or July, the NS had appointed a person to take charge of the labor draft, and this person seemed determined to make it work. Together with the so-called "Major-General" who was head of NS's State Police, he took measures to have everyone arrested who did not respond to the draft. He set up his headquarters at 8 Park Road, and soon had quite an archive there. We then received orders to deal with it. It proved impossible to get keys to the house, we couldn't even pick the lock, and we had to go there late one evening and batter the door down.

The noise of glass shattering as we broke in caused a good many windows to be flung up in the neighboring houses. To cover us—and get the heads drawn in—I bellowed: "Look out! It's drunken Germans and they're shooting!" Then we chucked a charge into the offices and ran. The charge went off all right, though it did not do a great deal of damage. However the offices were out of operation for a bit and the adventure had a considerable propaganda effect. Unfortunately, some of the damage it did was highly unwelcome. The Wine and Spirit Monopoly had a shop in the same building, and a good deal of its stock was damaged.

At the end of August we received orders from England to blow up a locomotive of the Thamshavn railway which was in Oslo being repaired. The Germans had lost their supplies of sulphur from Sicily and our pyrites from Orka were of considerable importance to their war effort. London wanted to cut off the Norwegian supplies.

For two years the NORIC men had made repeated attacks on the locomotives which drew the ore trains from the mines to the coast, because this track was a different gauge and the locomotives were irreplaceable. In one such attack, five of the locomotives were put out of action, and it was one of these that had been sent to Oslo for repair. This was the locomotive we were to deal with for it was the only one the Germans had any hope of repairing. In Oslo, the men in the repair shops did their best to sabotage the work, but the Germans were pressing for the job to be finished. They wanted that locomotive very badly.

At this time, I had good contacts in industry, one of whom got me an introduction to a man in Brown Boveri, the factory where the locomotive was being repaired. The same factory made repairs for the electric controls for the Thamshavn locomotives. My contact was able to give me all the information I needed about the locomotive. Even so, I felt we weren't ready to attempt the job, and I advised England that it was too early.

A little later in September, one of my contacts told me that orders had come from the Reichskommissariat that the locomotive must be repaired "at once." A night shift was ordered by the Germans to speed things.

The Thamshavn locomotive—without its wheels—was perched on a giant transporter of the Norwegian State Railways. Two companions and I studied the layout from the drawings and sketches our contacts had given us, then made a cautious reconnaissance of our own. Word came that the locomotive might be ready any day and that we must do the job quickly, if we were going to do it at all.

On midnight of September 12, I walked out of my hideout to meet Rasmussen and Tallaksen. The three of us had decided to deal with the locomotive. As I emerged, an air-raid alarm sounded. Fortunately, I was able to telephone my men and put off the attempt. There was no point in risking arrest by the Germans for being in the streets during an alert.

I had forty winks before the all-clear sounded. At one o'clock I set out again. Twenty minutes later, the three of us bicycled off to Bygdoy where the repair shop was, maintaining a distance between us so as not to be conspicuous.

The night watchmen at the repair shop were not a danger. They were ordinary Norwegian workmen compelled to act as anti-sabotage guards, and there were only four or five of them. But if they surprised us, the subsequent parleying would surely be heard by the Germans, who had patrols out in the neighborhood. There were two German guards on a gas station which was just opposite the Skabo works, though on the far side of a railway line. There were also two sentries who patrolled between the railway bridge and the industrial estate. And there was a large German camp nearby. Thus we had to reckon with German sentries or patrols passing nearby several times during the night.

We lay in a ditch by the roadside, close to the fence around the factory for a good ten minutes. We listened to locate the sentries and the route they took. When the sentries seemed to be farthest from us we cut the barbed-wire along the ditch and crawled through. All was quiet. I got a leg up, climbed over, and dropped into the factory area. The way seemed clear. The other two men followed quickly.

It was pitch dark and hard to get our bearings. We had to cross a gravelled space. Fortunately, a train came along and we took the opportunity to sprint across to the factory building. According to our information, the factory door was supposed to be open; it was shut.

We found a little side door which led us into a huge bay, from which we made our way into the locomotive bay. This was well lighted and the locomotive was standing where we'd expected to find it. Our plan was to use eight pounds of plastic to cut through the girder supporting one side of the locomotive and twist the locomotive's frame. In addition, we placed two three-pound charges to damage the controls.

While the others fixed the charges, I watched the door. Finally, after what seemed an eternity, the fuses were lit. We had two minutes to get out.

The lights in the bay were so bright that we were blinded when we walked out into the dark. We knew that we had to skirt a big turntable in the open space outside, but we couldn't see a thing. Rasmussen went a bit too far to the right and fell head first into the turntable pit. I heard him cry out and switched on my torch to see if he had hurt himself.

It was a six-foot drop, but he had managed to fall in about the only place which wasn't bristling with iron spikes and he was all right, except that he'd hurt an arm.

The third member of our party, Tallaksen, had turned back in the hope of being in time to tear away the bomb fuses. There was only half a minute to go before the blast and what he intended was tantamount to suicide. I managed to stop him. Rasmussen somehow clambered out on his own, and we got him over the two fences.

We jumped on our bicycles and hadn't gone ten yards when the charges went off, and the doors in the building were blown out. A few yards further, there was a narrow side road down which we turned. We got away from the area unscathed and bicycled back to the hideout. As we pedaled, we heard automobiles tearing towards the workshops.

We learned that the charge had done its job properly. It had taken a good eighteen inches out of the side-girder and the controls were useless.

Rasmussen had broken his wrist, but two days later he was out on another job with the wrist in a cast.

CHAPTER XX

Kongsberg Arms Factory

At the end of August we were instructed to have a preliminary look at two munition factories—one at Raufoss, the other at Kongsberg—fifty miles or so to the southwest of Oslo. London wanted both put out of action. It was not intended to raze the buildings to the ground, but to prevent their functioning for a considerable length of time.

We decided that Birger Rasmussen would deal with the Raufoss factory and I with the one at Kongsberg. First, we had to find out as much as we could about our targets. I got in touch with Beck, the head Milorg man at Kongsberg. I discovered that he came from my home town, Rjukan, and I knew him. He had long wanted to put the munitions factory out of action. His plan was to cut off the factory's supply of electricity by destroying its three transformers. I asked him to give me specific details but he came back very disappointed and told me that the Germans now had spare transformers at the power station. These were continuously guarded by a German with a machine gun. The project looked somewhat hopeless. There were civilian watchmen as well, which would make it pretty impossible to get near the place without running into somebody.

The watchmen were ordinary people pressed into service, but however decent they might be at heart, they couldn't be anything but a hindrance where we were concerned. I asked Beck to reconnoiter further.

Meanwhile, when Rasmussen came back from Raufoss, he had much the same story to tell. To stop the supply of current to that factory, we would have to destroy seven transformers, located in three different places. Also the guard at the factory had been strengthened after our recent sabotage, and consisted of fifteen Germans and several Norwegian watchmen with dogs. At the transformer station there was a Norwegian guard with an alarm apparatus.

We agreed that a direct attack on Raufoss would call for more people than we could muster. I consulted my contacts in industry. They put their heads together with various experts and advised that the best thing we could do would be to blow up a number of the pylons carrying the high-tension cable from Nore across Minnesund to Raufoss through Hurdalen. If we also blew up the transformer at Minnesund, which would be very difficult to replace, the whole factory would come to a stop or its output would be greatly restricted. This was the job Rasmussen went off to do with his wrist still in a cast.

Beck was an energetic fellow and in the middle of September he came to Oslo with another plan. The arms factory at Kongsberg was an important producer of Bofors AA-guns, made under license. The factory's capacity was around thirty guns a month but, as every man Jack there did his best to sabotage production, it had never been higher than about five a month. The factory also repaired larger guns, and at this time there were four Bofors AA-guns ready for dispatch and a big 15 cm. field gun being repaired. Experts had told Beck that if we could destroy the two big boring-and-drilling machines, it would halt production for a long time. If we used big enough charges for this, there was a good chance that we would damage the structure of the building as well.

All the civilian watchmen had been withdrawn, but there was still a considerable military guard on the place. Usually the guard consisted of Germans, both by day and at night, but at the moment the watch was being maintained by the Norwegian Waffen SS. This was a guard battalion especially trained by the Germans. The head of this battalion was reputed to have said that neither God nor the Devil would be able to get into the Kongsberg Arms Factory while *he* was guarding it, and this had stuck in the throat of the Milorg man who, I could see, was dying to be allowed to take part in the action. But that was not for me to decide.

The factory security was well organized. A patrol of three men armed with machine-guns was in the factory area all night. Once an hour, an ordinary night-watchman made the rounds. These night-watchmen had dogs. They were decent people, but that would be no help if the dogs gave the show away. And if there was any incident the watchmen didn't report to the Germans, they would undoubtedly suffer. The same thing went for the fire patrol that passed the factory every forty minutes.

With this knowledge, I took Beck to discuss the project with Jens Chr. Hauge. First came the question of how many men I would need for such a difficult undertaking. Beck mentioned that he was familiar with local conditions and also that he had a good man in Milorg who actually worked in the factory and was familiar with the whole factory area. Hauge saw what he was hinting at. However, it was against every rule for a Milorg commander to take part in such actions. Hauge then asked him if he thought it would be a risky job, and was told that the man didn't think it would be dangerous at all. I could hardly agree with the Kongsberg man, but I kept quiet. All I said was that if he particularly wanted to be in on the job, I thought it would be a good idea if he were. At that, Hauge gave his assent.

The matter was then referred to SOE and Norwegian authorities in London. They agreed to the attempt being made. The final plan was laid by Beck and me. Beck and his factory contact, Gundeid, were not to be armed and, if we were surprised, were to escape if they could. I was to carry a machine-pistol with a silencer and my usual .38 colt. Gundeid, who had to get back to his home that night, was to use a bicycle, which would also prevent his being tracked by dogs. Beck was to return to Oslo after the job was done.

It was essential that the job appear not to have been carried out by Milorg or local people because the Germans would retaliate against the civilian population; so we were to leave behind bits of English uniform and equipment to persuade the Germans the deed was done by British parachutists.

On September 17 I got into our Chevrolet. On its windscreen was a paper informing all who might be concerned that the car was the property of the Roads and Highways Department and was permitted to go anywhere in southern Norway. My cover story was that I was a consulting engineer and on my way to Numedal to look at a road that we feared would slip down the mountain-side. Under the seat I had an unusual piece of civil engineer's equipment; a machine-pistol. It was unusual having a big silencer screwed onto the end of the barrel—a bulbous affair about sixteen inches long—but it effectively muffled the reports. The car also was unusual, because it had a special fitting whereby, even when it was running on gasoline, a small fan maintained the draught in the gas generator so that the outside felt normally warm to the touch. My identity card was issued in Oslo under the name of Haugen, and I also had another (which Beck had provided) which bore the stamp of the Kongsberg police. The controls around Kongsberg were so strict that any outsider would be sharply questioned, if he was stopped driving into the town in the evening.

I had arranged to meet Beck outside Kongsberg at a point where the road dipped down towards the town itself. There was a little side road leading to the right, and I turned the car and parked it there. It was three o'clock in the afternoon. Beck and I walked into the town, where we had a meal at the house of one of his contacts. (It was best to avoid restaurants.) At five o'clock we met Gundeid and he led us across the lower bridge. On the far side the explosives were hidden, already packed in rucksacks, two hundred and fifty pounds of plastic that Milorg had got from England in one of the arms drops.

We collected the rucksacks and went to a barn in a field by the factory area only a short distance from the office block. We had plenty of time, so I leisurely prepared the charges, with the others' help. We made four three-pound charges for the four Bofors guns and one ten-pound charge for the big field-gun, and a 100-pound charge for the drill and boring machine. That was an enormous charge, of course, but we wanted to damage the structure of the building as well. One more charge remained, 115 pounds for the second boring-machine. But where was the explosive?

I could scarcely believe my ears when Gundeid told me it was already inside the factory, in the assembly bay. Gundeid worked at a lathe in the gallery of the big hall and had been daring or foolhardy enough to take small quantities of explosive in with him in his lunch bag and hide it near his lathe. To prevent any of the guards looking into his bag, he had hung it on a hook in the fence while he put his bicycle away. Then, having passed through the guards, he walked along the fence and retrieved his bag without anyone noticing. It was all very admirable, of course, but it made things difficult for me. To put the charge together in the factory itself would mean being in there five to ten minutes longer than we had planned, and then the two charges had to be linked with cordtex fuse. However there was nothing to be done but get going and hope to be able to work undisturbed.

By nine o'clock the charges were ready. It was pitch dark. We crept up to the fence and lay on our stomachs to wait. At ten o'clock the night watchmen went past on their round. It was a relief when waiting time was over, for the night was raw and cold. Beck was still in thin summer things, but did not let it bother him. I could see that we all were feeling the tension.

I had a special pair of pliers with which I cut the chain on the first gate. This took a small bite out of a link, just large enough to let one slip it free and put it back in place afterwards without any passerby noticing that it had been cut. We dared not go off the roads in the factory area, because the area was mined. We had a key to the next gate, so it should have been simpler, but when we tried to lock it behind us, we couldn't get the key to turn. That was an unexpected snag, but there was nothing to be done. If a night watchman came past while we were inside, the gate could arouse his suspicions. We had no choice but to hope the watchmen would not be particularly observant.

Gundeid then led us to a back door in the machining bay. Again we had a key, but I took out a knife and made a few scratches on the Yale lock to make it look as though it had been picked. The lights were all on in the vast building, and it looked like a great ballroom, though of course the windows were blacked out. We saw at once that there would be little chance of hiding, if anyone came along while we were there. The bright lights, too, would make connecting the charges and camouflaging the long fuses even more of a nervous strain. Fuses had to be camouflaged, for we were planning a four-hour delay on the fuses, and the whole plan would be spoiled if the night watchmen should discover any of the linking fuses in the meantime. The four hours were to allow one hour's walk back to the car, two hours' drive to Oslo, and one hour in reserve.

I stood by the main door with my machine-pistol ready, while the other two went up to the gallery where Gundeid's lathe and the explosive were. Ten suspenseful minutes passed while they made up the charge exactly as I had done with the others out in the barn. I was indeed glad when I saw them come down with the charge all ready so I could get to work. The strain was almost unbearable. It didn't take long to put the charges in place and link them together; the slow business was camouflaging the white cordtex fuses. (I resolved to complain to London about sending us white fuses, which were more difficult to conceal.) Fortunately we found a number of boards we could use as camouflage by moving them a little.

At exactly ten minutes to eleven I pressed home the pencil time-fuses and started off the chemical reaction. In four hours' time, more or less, the charges would explode.

Next we went to the assembly bay, where the guns were. It took us five minutes to lay the four charges in place, connect the fuses, camouflage them and press home the pencils. This bay was brilliantly lit too and it was far from easy to hide the fuses. Then we found that we hadn't quite enough cordtex to reach from the last Bofors gun to the big 15 cm field gun; so we laid the bits of cordtex as close together as we could, hoping for a "sympathetic detonation," as I had been taught by the experts in England.

We had now spent considerably longer in the factory than originally planned. Our luck, to the moment, had been fantastic. There hadn't been a sign of a patrol or night watchman. We stole out of the back door, locked it, and made our way to the gate in the inner fence. Here we saw a light some 200 yards away and realized that the guard was there. Gundeid took things calmly and made another attempt to lock the gate, but the lock still wouldn't budge. We learned later that, while we were inside, the patrol had come to the gate, seen it was not locked, and just thought that one of the night-watchmen had forgotten to lock it after him.

The last gate was easy. We replaced the chain behind us so that it appeared whole and undisturbed.

Gundeid mounted his bicycle at once, so the dogs would not find his tracks. Beck and I walked back up to the car. It was midnight when we started off. Just before we got to Drammen, there was a road block with armed police who searched the whole car but found nothing. I had left my machine-pistol behind in Kongsberg. The car's documents passed muster and I had no need to trot out my cover story. The charcoal generator was convincingly nice and warm. We reached Oslo about two o'clock, went to our hide-outs and I, at least, slept the sleep of the just well into Sunday.

That Sunday afternoon Gundeid came into Oslo by train to give us what news he had managed to glean. The charges had gone off earlier than we had calculated. As far as he could make out, the big charges had gone off at 2:15, those on the four Bofors guns at 2:30, and that on the field-gun at 2:45. The big charges had had an excellent effect, the 200-foot wall of the machining bay was down on the side facing the river.

One writer described our handiwork as follows:

"Some of the houses nearby had their windows blown in by the blast, and pieces of metal and bits of brick were scattered over a wide area. The first thought people had, once they had got themselves out of bed and into their clothes, was: Now the Arms factory's being bombed. Ever since the Germans had taken over the factory, there had been a succession of rumors that it was next on the list for the attentions of the Allied bombers, so when the first explosion literally shook people out of their beds, their natural reaction was that now it was happening. Gradually, as people learned what actually was going on, it was, in spite of everything, a relief. The fear of an air raid had been a constant threat hanging over the heads of those who lived anywhere near the factory. People had to assume that any bombing of the factory would entail death among their numbers as well as destruction of civilian property.

"The succession of explosions roaring in the darkness of the September night caused considerable tension and made us all feel apprehensive. After a bit, there were a lot of Germans at the factory, all fearfully excited and nervous. The streets were patrolled by large patrols armed with machine-pistols and hand-grenades, so that any who did not have compelling reasons to venture into the area did best to stay indoors."

The factory guards on duty that night were convinced there had been a large number of saboteurs at work, but otherwise couldn't explain what had happened or how. The bits of British uniform and equipment were found, and the Germans appeared to believe that the action had been carried out by Allied parachute troops. Our clandestine press quickly reported that saboteurs in British uniform had been at work.

So, we had done it. But what we did could never have been accomplished without Gundeid.

Later we heard of a gruesome conclusion to the story. The German investigators could not find any clues, but they had to have a scapegoat so they arrested a man who worked on one of the big boring machines we had blown up. He was interrogated in the usual Gestapo manner and beaten with cudgels and sticks. One eye was so badly damaged that he lost the use of it altogether. He was finally sent to Grini and kept there till the end of the war.

One Sunday morning I was at Mrs. Collett's flat, which I left later that afternoon. The next day one of my contacts told me Mrs. Collett had been trying to get in touch with me. She wasn't then at home, and I was told the State Police had been to her flat in a vain attempt to arrest her. Later that afternoon, I got in touch with her at one of my previous hideouts (which she had found for me) and went to see her. She looked all right, but I could see immediately that something had happened. And so it had!

That morning, just before eight o'clock her doorbell had rung. She hadn't been in any hurry to answer it and the ringing had persisted. Sensing that all was not well she had flung on a dressing gown and, as she did so, heard violent hammering on the front door. She stole out the back way, neatly shutting the door behind her, took a careful look around, and tiptoed down the back stairs. Having satisfied herself that there was no one outside the back door, she slipped out, bent double, and ran along between the side of the house and the fence separating the path from the street. There was a porch on the ground floor with some wood piled under it, and there she hid.

She stayed there for two or three hours. Then she crept inside to one of the ground-floor flats. Here she was told that two or three men had been making a noise on her landing. After a bit they had gone to the back stairs and then outside to confer with a man standing beside a car. They had all been in mufti. The woman had told Mrs. Collett it was pretty certain they were people from the State Police.

It was lucky for us that Mrs. Collett had escaped. She had worked in the underground movement since its beginnings, knew many of the

149

leading people in it, and was familiar with much of my work. It would have been ominous for us if she had been arrested. As it was, to be deprived of her wide network of contacts and acquaintances was a considerable loss to us, but she had to go into hiding. She hid for two weeks and then we got her across to Sweden.

The State Police put a guard in her flat as soon as they discovered she wasn't there—as Mrs. Andersen discovered. She had arranged to visit Mrs. Collett that same morning and of course walked up and rang the bell, unsuspecting. The door was opened by a man in street clothes. Instinct told her he was a policeman. The man asked if she had come to see Mrs. Collett. Mrs. Andersen was very quick-witted and she replied that she was collecting for the Church Bazaar and had come because Mrs. Collett always gave them something. She was so calm and assured that the man didn't doubt her and, after asking her a few more simple questions, he let her go. Fortunately, he was not one of those who had taken part in the State Police searches at Gronland Street, because the full address was on Mrs. Andersen's identity card.

Mrs. Andersen seemed unmoved by it all, but we felt that she and her daughter had now done their bit and that the time had come for them too to get over into Sweden. We had a feeling that the days of 30 Gronland Street were numbered.

All this time Mrs. Andersen had been running the bakery and its branches, a big undertaking, and we hoped that the Germans would not now move in and take over.

It was truly a miracle that we had been able to make such excellent use of 30 Gronland Street all those years. The Andersens had endured a lot for us. Many of us felt that we belonged to the family and we were bereft when Mrs. Andersen and her daughter had gone.

That summer of 1944 we had a sailing holiday on Oslo fjord! My Esso contact, Thorp, got himself a sailing permit from the Gestapo and so Birger Rasmussen, Edvard Tallaksen, I, and other lads from England were sailing about in a boat with the Gestapo's blessing! If only the Gestapo had known! There were not many boats out on the fjord that summer. The ordinary decent Norwegian would not ask a favor of the Gestapo or any other German, and a sailing permit was such a favor. As far as we were concerned, it could only be a good thing if we were regarded as tainted or semi-collaborationist. That was an excellent reputation for resistance workers to have!

We lost a number of people at this time. One of our Esso people was arrested and Thorp had to go into hiding. Two others had to go to Sweden, taking their families with them.

We now had a sort of headquarters at 6 Hertzberg Street. Both Morland and I spent the night there on various occasions, and we often held meetings there. Later in the autumn of 1944 Thorp (now back out of hiding) told us that he had met a young woman whom he believed to be working for the Germans. He had heard from other sources that she was working for a Gestapo member Weiner, who had a network of informers acting for him. The young woman had confirmed this and told Thorp she could see that the war was going to end the wrong way for the Germans and she asked to be allowed to help the Resistance Movement so as to get off lightly when the war was over.

We mistrusted the offer, but after a great amount of discussion it was decided that I should interview her. I arranged to meet her at her room, and I must admit to feeling pretty unsafe as she ushered me in and seated me opposite her. After some talk, however, I began to feel that perhaps she really was in earnest; even so I was glad when I was back on the street again, after having arranged a one-way contact—by which I could reach her, but not she me. She was later visited again through a contact, and investigations showed that what she had told me was all true. In the end, we profited quite a lot by information she gave us. Among other things, she tipped us off that the Germans were becoming interested in Hertzberg Street, though they had not yet found out names or address.

We still had several safe routes across Norway into Sweden. One was provided by the lifeboat service, where Captain Holter did sterling work for us. He took our people out in a lifeboat and landed them by row boat on the Swedish coast. On one such trip he had four of the Home Front chiefs with him, all going to Stockholm for a conference. Before this, when Hauge wanted to go to Stockholm, we used to put him into the locker of an Esso tank truck and drive him by the shortest route to the frontier.

I was now having regular meetings with the Central Committee. They had started a sham building firm called Holatex, with offices at the top of a big block in Sorgenfri Street. The people in the building thought them what we called "barracks-kings," people who built camps for the Germans.

A joiner had made a secret cavity in the floor, where they kept firearms in case of unwelcome visitors. I instructed them in their use, but fortunately they never had to demonstrate whether I had taught them well or not.

CHAPTER XXI

A Big Blaze

Our group from England now acquired a nickname: to the Central Committee we were called the Oslo Gang. Meanwhile Milorg had been going in for sabotage of oil and gasoline stores and been very successful. At the beginning of October we learned that the Germans had a big store of grease and lubricating oil down in the docks. This included a quantity of special gear oil. We were told to destroy the store.

The Germans' arrangements for guarding the store were peculiar. At night the place was alive with German sentries and patrols, yet during the day apparently there wasn't a single guard or sentry on duty. Apart from the fact that Germans were always driving past as they went to and from the various parts of the docks, the place seemed unguarded.

The most difficult thing about the job was to get the synthetic oil to burn. To accomplish this we needed gasoline and incendiary bombs. Six of us were to do the job—Tallaksen, Rasmussen, Manus, Gram, Houlder, and me. Unfortunately Manus had had a shooting accident and had been wounded in the chest and thigh. He looked pretty pale about the gills although he was pronounced well enough to drive the Nash.

Our plan was this: At 9:45 in the morning we would set off in the Nash with Manus driving, Tallaksen beside him, and me on the flat together with two sixty-gallon drums of gasoline, a pile of incendiaries, and a number of two and a half pound charges of plastic explosive. The other three were to follow on bicycles a short distance behind.

One of our main difficulties was the incredible efficiency of the Oslo fire brigade, which usually reached the scene of any outbreak far too quickly for our purpose. We had good friends in the Fire Brigade and we discussed the matter with them. They were all good patriots, but they couldn't delay going to a fire to any noticeable extent nor could they appear halfhearted in their work. However, we managed to concoct a plan to prevent them reaching the scene of our fire in time to do any real good. Some of our group were to make false alarms all over the city just as ours was due to break; thus the fire engines would be scattered all over the city.

On Thursday, October 12, at 9:45 a.m. we drove out from our garage. There was thick mist over the docks and it was raining steadily. Our intention was to drive straight to Sorenga, where the store was, and up to the store itself. There I would jump off the truck, and go into the office and hold up the clerks and any visitors who might come in.

As usual, there was a surprise in store for us. As we reached the part of the docks where the store was, we caught sight of a German truck with about fifteen soldiers sitting nearby. Manus, who was driving, had very quick reactions and, instead of turning in, he drove on further up the docks. After a bit we stopped, and Tallaksen and I jumped off and walked back to see if there was any sign of the Germans leaving. After a tedious half-hour wait, we saw them get in and drive off. Tallaksen and I walked into the store office. There was nobody. We went into the store, where we found four men. Politely, Tallaksen asked them to put their hands up and keep away from the telephone. Then I took them into the office for a little chat. Tallaksen signaled to Manus, who drove up and in. The others followed quickly on their bicycles and went to work.

We had to be quick, because the four store workers told us that the Germans intended to return for some of the oil. Charges were fixed to four oil-drums, and connected with an exploding fuse. The incendiary bombs were scattered along the line of the fuse, but a little away from it; then the gasoline was poured over the whole thing and the truck was

154

driven out. While we were doing this, Max Manus went around photographing the Oslo gang at work. (Not one of the pictures came out!) We also fixed a charge to the fire hydrant at the store, to put that out of action. Then we started a five-minute fuse, and I sent the four workers marching off towards Sorenga.

The explosion was quite effective. Despite all our precautions, the fire brigade did get there before destruction was complete. However, 50,000 gallons of oil were burned as was a considerable quantity of special gear oil. The building was ruined. The Germans had to move what oil was left.

It was a source of constant amazement for Per Morland and me that neither of us had got caught and that we always managed to get through the control points, of which there seemed to be more and more. We were always changing our names and once this had led to difficulties—because we had both chosen the same name. Not only that, but we were staying at the same place, the Gynecological Clinic, where consequently we were known as Knudsen 1 and Knudsen 2. After this we conferred before choosing a new name for our identity cards.

One day when Morland was out with the van, it broke down. He telephoned and asked me to come with the truck and tow him away. I got there as quickly as I could, we tied on the tow rope and I drove off, but unfortunately I started with a jerk that sent the two vehicles bumping into each other. People stopped and must have wondered why the two young drivers thought it so funny to have banged into each other. When we had recovered enough to be able to drive, we got in again, and again I started off with a jerk and again we collided. Then we could hardly drive for laughing. It was a miracle we ever got away.

One day when Morland was crossing the main thoroughfare of Kirkeveien, a German on a motor-bicycle rode full tilt into him. Morland was too far out in the middle to avoid him; the German went hurtling over the hood and landed on his head on the other side. He lay sprawling there in rather a mess. Morland felt it expedient to vanish and hurried off, leaving his car. That evening we heard that the Traffic Police had towed Morland's car away and that it was in their garage. As far as our informant knew, it was perfectly roadworthy. The accident, of course, had caused a bit of a stir, because the police had discovered that there was something peculiar about the car's papers. They were excellent fakes but the details did not agree with the central register, which showed that the State Grain Board did not possess any such car.

The next day, Morland and I went to the police garage. There was our car all right, standing out in the open space. There wasn't a soul to be seen, not a guard or anyone. We walked in as if the place belonged to us, got into the car, and drove out. We took the car straight to "our" garage, where it was re-sprayed a lovely gray color and given a set of nice new number plates.

CHAPTER XXII

London and Lunch with King Haakon of Norway

On October 9, Per Morland and I set out for Stockholm again. This time we decided to let ourselves be taken across by one of the "exporters." It was our first experience in this form of travel and I rather dreaded having to entrust myself to others, instead of using our own well-tried organization.

Our orders were to go to Grefsen, a suburban station. There, at one o'clock in the morning, we got into a brake-van of a train and made contact with the guard. We stayed in the train as far as Skarnes, where we met a man with a truck, who drove us some distance east. Like all other refugees who used these routes, we had no idea what was happening.

At six o'clock we found ourselves tramping east, but later on we turned north. Then we realized we were following the frontier, keeping away from paths and roads as far as possible. All day we walked. It was heavy going across the bog and through bushes. Our guide was an elderly forester, but we found it difficult to keep up with him. Eventually we got fed up with going north all the time, and couldn't see why we didn't head for the frontier.

At about eight or nine that night we finally reached a hamlet, where a young fellow took over from our elderly forester. A short while later, we crossed the railway and a road. Then we realized where we were!

We had got to Abogen, between Kongsvinger and Austmarka. We thought we knew this part of the country well enough to manage the rest on our own. The boy recommended a man to us who agreed to drive us to Ostgarden and by half-past ten we were with the Skoglunds at Tomta. Their son—the one who had joined the Nazi Party for us—had come under suspicion and had to flee to Sweden, so his parents felt as though they were sitting on a volcano. Nonetheless, we spent the night there at Tomta and the next morning we got in contact with Engelbrektsson, our friendly Swedish customs man, and he passed us on to the people at Charlottenberg, where we reported as fully as we could about conditions in Norway and the morale of the Germans in Oslo and the like. Then we boarded a train and rode to Stockholm.

It was fun to meet old friends again. Many of those who had had to escape to Sweden were gathered together in Stockholm. It was not an ideal life, and understandably some of these refugees were disgruntled. There were a number of camps now where they could be trained, and jobs were easy to find. Here I met SOE's Stockholm chief, Tom Nielsen, or Uncle (his cover-name and also his nickname). He was a grand fellow and I came to think very highly of him. He now had a replacement for Mrs. Waring, a girl from Bergen who later married Max Manus. His new assistant's cover-name was "Aunt," as Mrs. Waring's had been.

We wrote reports about our work in Norway and attended conferences about projected future actions in Norway. We had meetings at the Military Office and met some of Milorg's people there and of course went to the refugee screening office.

When I had been in Stockholm some weeks I received orders to go to England, but I was told that I would be back in Stockholm well before Christmas, and could return to Oslo in January. There was plenty to be done in Oslo now, and I did not want to be away long—especially as Morland had already gone back after a very brief holiday.

On November 14, 1944, I boarded the plane to fly to England again. To my surprise, one of my fellow passengers was Jens Chr. Hauge, but we had to pretend we didn't even know one another.

London looked no worse than it had in 1943. There were still plenty of bomb-craters and, though the V1's had stopped coming—the British having learned how to shoot them down—the V2's had started, coming like lightning out of a clear sky. One of them fell in Oxford Street a few days after my arrival and the blast was so violent that it shook my bed in the Cumberland Hotel. It was unbelievable how calmly the British took this.

I was well received by SOE and our Norwegian FO4 and was sent to the best known of their training schools, STS 17, where the advanced sabotage courses were held. Now I was not a student but a lecturer on our experiences in the practical use of different explosives, laying charges, etc. I enjoyed that.

I met many of the British chiefs on this occasion. I particularly liked Major Boughton-Leigh, who with Martin Linge, had started the Scandinavian Section in 1940. He took me in his car to the school, and we talked about Linge and the development of Norwegian Independent Company No. 1. I told him something of my difficulties when I was in England before, and pointed out how easy it was for them—or for us—to judge each other wrongly, at all events in individual cases. I mentioned Axelssen's case pointing out that this was the man responsible for the *Bismarck* report. The major pricked up his ears and asked where Axelssen was. He became even more eager to help when I said that I would like to take Axelssen back home with me.

The point here was that we needed new people for Oslo. The day I reached London I heard that Tallaksen and Gram had walked into a trap in Oslo. They had gone to meet two German *agents provocateurs* at a cafe. The Gestapo had been sitting there waiting. Ten or twelve of them opened fire. Gram was killed and Tallaksen was badly wounded. He was taken under guard to Aker Hospital.

That sad news took all the pleasure out of my first few days in London. I had to replace these men and FO4 and SOE agreed to my selecting two whom they would fly across to Oslo district and drop there. I was delighted when I learned that I could get Axelssen.

In London I came across a bitter man who returned from a job in Norway and had not been used again. His brother had been killed at Trondheim, and he hated that he was inactive. He felt this was because he had criticized certain people. I could sympathize with his urge to get back and fight. Right or wrong, it wasn't easy to have to kick one's heels in England when there was work to do at home. I liked this man, Pevik, and suggested him as the second man for Oslo. Both FO4 and SOE agreed, so that was settled.

Another man called Norman Gabrielsen, Pevik, and I, who had all worked in Norway for long periods, discovered that we had accumulated a nice sum in our bank accounts in England, for we were paid while we were working in Norway. There was little point in saving the money and none in squandering it, so we decided to start a fund for NORIC I. We scraped together what we had—almost 9000 Crowns. Little by little the fund became known among the NORIC I people and the idea took hold and was developed and expanded in Norway after the war.

After some days in London, I went up to Scotland to see what the training was like then at Glenmore. They had built a number of huts there and Forest Lodge had been handed over to the Americans. People from the Army and Navy had come for training, with NORIC people acting as instructors. It was time to set up bases in Norway, and training for this was in full swing.

Back in London I had discussed with FO4 and SOE what job I was to do when I got back to Oslo. After a few days of detailed briefing I was ready to leave. But before I went I had the honor of a lengthy audience with King Haakon and Crown Prince Olav, who was then Chief of Staff. Both were intensely interested in our work and very well informed.

I had had a previous audience with the King when I was in London in 1943. I shall never forget those two meetings. On the second occasion I went with the King and his adjutant to lunch at the Carlton. That was the first time in my life—and the last—to see each and every guest in a large dining room stand up and bow.

Towards the end of the meal, Colonel Nordie, King Haakon's adjutant, had to go, leaving the King alone with me. We chatted for a while. The King's spirit and humor were infectious.

While in London I met an old friend, Fridtjof Hoyer of Esso in Oslo. He was now a major in the Air Force and he was on leave. I also met Georg Vetlesen, head of the Scandinavian section of the OSS. Where Scandinavia was concerned, the Americans were late in appearing on the scene, but once they were there, they made their presence felt. Because of all the equipment needed for the Second Front, the British had difficulty in supplying NORIC I. Vetlesen now appeared with OSS's vast resources, which soon provided all that NORIC I required.

I was intrigued to see how cautious all departments concerned with the Occupied Territories were. Security was strictly enforced, as I found to my cost. All my meetings had taken place at various offices, but never at SOE headquarters, for it was believed that the Germans would be very interested in knowing where in London it was located. By mistake I was taken there once, and Colonel Wilson was hopping mad at this breach of regulation.

My orders were now ready. They were headed: DIRECTIVE TO NO. 24. They said, among other things:

"No. 24 is attached to the Central Committee of the Home Forces as their sabotage leader, and all operations he carries out will be performed under orders of the Central Committee or direct orders from London received through the Committee."

Then I was given a directive listing the objects of special importance which should be attacked.

This time I did not have to wait months or even weeks to cross the North Sea. It was no easier to get a seat in the Norwegian-English planes to Stockholm, but now the Americans had started an air transport of arms and equipment for the Norwegian police troops being trained in Sweden in the various refugee camps. (The Swedes had finally given their permission to form these so-called police units, which could be employed when the situation in Norway made their presence essential to maintain law and order.) They were, of course, more than just police; they were proper military formations set up by decree of the Norwegian Government in December, 1943. The Government's great headache had been the equipment for these troops, but now the Americans had come into the picture and the Swedes permitted their big Liberator Transport planes to land equipment. Things were moving rapidly.

It was with one of these American transports that I took off from Halesworth on Friday, December 15. We landed safely at Bromma outside Stockholm later that night, where "Uncle" and "Aunt" and Sverre Ellingsen were waiting to give me the latest news from Oslo. I had left just six weeks before.

CHAPTER XXIII

An Unpleasant Trip

Four days after I returned to Stockholm, I was told that Arne Diesen had been arrested by the State Police. This was a shock, because Diesen knew a great deal about our organization and if he was made to talk our activities would be considerably curtailed. I immediately sent a message to Morland in Oslo asking him to find out why Diesen had been arrested. There was no great difficulty in this, thanks to our friends in the State Police, and it wasn't long before Morland replied that Diesen had been arrested in connection with a travel permit. He had been seen handing over a permit to one of my contacts, but had managed to twist out of it by pretending that he was dealing in the black market for food.

There was no getting away from the disturbing knowledge that there was a very weak security link in our organization. This wasn't the first incident.

Uncle and Aunt told me that after Gregers Gram had been killed and Tallaksen captured, the rest of the Oslo Gang had been depressed. They hadn't been able to get Tallaksen out of Aker Hospital before he was moved to the prison hospital, and they had been afraid the Germans with their notorious torture methods might be able to force him—a sick and wounded man—to talk. To be on the safe side, they had all moved to new hideouts.

However, no one needed to worry where Tallaksen was concerned. He took his own life in prison. It was, perhaps, only what one might have predicted. He could expect nothing of the Germans except death by torture. He had shown his determination not to be taken alive at Whitsun, 1944, when he had hidden under some steps, ready to draw out the pin from a hand grenade if the Germans discovered him.

None of us, if arrested in Oslo now, could do anything else but what Tallaksen did, if we were to save the organization and the vital interests of the resistance movement. But I had been impressed by the fact that after the business with Gram and Tallaksen the rest of the group had spirit enough to carry out another assignment. Led by Rasmussen they had destroyed SKF's store of ball-bearings, a good sixty tons of them, just before the Germans were to requisition them. They did the job with real precision. The SKF building was destroyed, yet none of the adjacent houses was damaged.

The death of Gram and Tallaksen increased my impatience to get back to Oslo. But Christmas was at hand and it was decided that I should stay in Stockholm until the New Year.

This time I was to travel along an entirely new route, one which was considered pretty safe, even if you had a lot of baggage—as I had—a suitcase full of arms and special equipment. I was to travel to Gothenburg and along the Swedish coast and out to Koster, an island off the coast where one of the refugee boats from Notteroy would pick me up and take me back on its return trip.

I left Gothenburg on January 17 and by the next day was safely installed in a fisherman's little house out on Koster. There the fishermen were helpful and perfectly familiar with the refugee boats from Notteroy. The boat from Notteroy which was to take me back had been delayed several days and had experienced a dramatic voyage. The weather had been stormy all week and it was a tough struggle to force passage with a big cargo of refugees below deck. The engine had broken down and for a time the boat had drifted where the storm chose to take it. Fortunately, there was no sign of a patrol boat. The two-man crew had been hard at it for fifty-six hours, and the refugees hadn't an easy time either. The sea has never appealed to me greatly, even when calm, and I shuddered at having to set out in such weather. I had no choice: I had to return to Oslo as soon as I could. The storm was increasing instead of abating, and it was many degrees below freezing.

The stern sheets of the boat were open and covered with ice. It was almost impossible to stay on one's feet.

Weather or no weather, we sailed on Friday evening. Soon waves were smashing over the tiny boat, and I had to lend a hand and pump, even though I soon was sick as a dog. The engine was in trouble again and the two men couldn't keep it running for long at a time. But they never turned a hair and their example inspired me—or shamed me—into pulling myself together—or as much as my seasickness allowed.

We were making little headway against the storm, and it became obvious that we couldn't get across under the cover of darkness. To sail those waters in daylight was to invite a visit from a German patrol boat and that meant capture. When daylight came, they hove to in the ice of a rocky island. As far as I could make out, we were at Store Faerder—about half way across. It was no haven. The three of us were soaked and it was piercingly cold. Somehow the day passed.

As soon as it was dark again (it being mid-January, darkness came early in the afternoon) we set sail for Notteroy. Towards evening the motor began giving more than its usual trouble. It kept stopping and, as we were now getting close to land, these stoppages were most unnerving. Every time the motor stopped we drifted closer and closer and more than once I thought we were going to crash among the breakers. It was obviously no mere breeze we were out in, but a full-fledged winter's storm. Luck was with us, however, and every time it seemed that all was over, my shipmates got the motor going again. But how I regretted not having gone over land! Even with the storm, the greatest danger was the risk of being caught by a German patrol boat. Both of my companions had pistols. I had a couple of machine-pistols in my suitcase. All of these weren't much against a German boat.

We had battled the sea for more than twenty-four hours. The two boatmen had set out on the return trip without rest and it was a miracle that they kept going. When we at last were approaching our destination, it dawned on me with surprise that we had a chance of getting there after all. How the two managed to find their way in the pitch darkness was beyond my comprehension.

As day was dawning, we got into calm water. Shortly afterwards we tied up at the coal merchant's jetty on Notteroy. The coal merchant's family gave me a wonderful welcome and I stayed with them till the afternoon, when someone with a car gave me a lift into Tonsberg.

Here I caught a train for Oslo. It was Sunday evening and the train was full so I had to dump my suitcases in the corridor and leave them to look after themselves. We reached Oslo fairly late in the evening. I phoned Morland at once and he came to drive me to one of our common hideouts.

The remnants of the Oslo Gang were hatching a plan with some of the Milorg people for setting fire to another oil dump, this time in the center of the city. The plans were complete and the attempt was to be made the following day, January 23. It was a relief to find that they had all the men they needed, for I had no particular wish to leap straight into such an action without time to get used to the feel of Oslo again.

Where I was staying that night—my old hideout the Gynecological Clinic—was only a block from the oil store and I heard the explosion and looked out of the window. Judging from the resultant fire, the action had gone off very well.

I was soon in touch with the Central Committee and discussed the assignments I had been given in London. The Oslo situation was even more difficult now. There were far more control-points in the streets and the Germans had patrols out checking identity cards. The German-trained Norwegian Nazi patrols were becoming offensive, and it was not as easy talking yourself free of them as it was of the Germans. They carried rifles now and were not to be joked with. Also as a rule, they went about in packs of eight or ten. They went systematically through brief cases and bicycle baskets and thoroughly searched the cars they stopped. Even so, it was easiest to get away if you were driving a car. For some reason they were impressed by people in their own cars, and so our ordinary private cars were now the safest ones to use. These still had State Police numbers, and we always used our Police identity cards when stopped by these creatures.

CHAPTER XXIV

In the Lion's Jaws

I was soon back in the swing again, meeting daily with Morland, the Oslo Gang, the Milorg people, and, of course, my friends in Holatex. I don't know what they would have done if the Germans had asked them to build barracks or huts. Perhaps we would have made our fortunes if we had started earlier and gone in for it properly!

It was incredible how many close shaves those fellows had. Time and time again they had bluffed and got away from the Nazis, saved as often as not by the false bottoms in their brief cases and secret pockets in their billfolds.

At about the time of my return Arthur Pevik and Viggo Axelssen arrived safely from London. A big American Liberator dropped them together with a quantity of arms and equipment for us to use in Oslo. Included were some coveted Piat guns. Till then there had never been any to spare us. The Piat is a baby cannon. About three feet long and weighing 35 pounds, it can shoot a 90 mm. grenade a hundred yards. It could knock holes in a tank and we felt that we really were capable of something now.

We soon had use for Axelssen's services, sooner perhaps than he had expected. In February I was asked to reinforce the saboteurs south of Oslo and act as their instructor. The objectives in and around Horten, the naval station, were very important. I had more than enough to do in Oslo and couldn't get away, so I suggested to the Central Committee that our best man for explosives was Birger Rasmussen, and that it would be a good idea if one of the new men from England went too. Morland got hold of a big Chrysler with a carbide generator for them. It ran on gasoline, of course, but the generator was good camouflage.

Rasmussen and Axelssen were to take arms and sabotage equipment with them in the car, which was fitted with a State Police number. There was, of course, always a risk of running into the State Police in Oslo but some risks had to be taken.

On March 6 the two were ready. Some time after eleven o'clock they drove to the Shell gas station, where one of the attendants used to let us have gas. This man had gone off somewhere for a moment and, while waiting for him, Rasmussen and Axelssen went for a stroll down the street. All at once they saw a patrol of Hirden's Nazi guards coming along. Rasmussen and Axelssen were armed and they could not risk being stopped and searched. They turned down a side street and hoped to get away unnoticed, but they just walked into a trap, for the street was a blind alley. At the bottom they sought refuge in the staircase of the last building. Rasmussen drew his pistol and stood with it half hidden behind his back.

Three of the patrol had followed them, and they soon appeared on the stair, rifles at the ready. Rasmussen opened fire and dropped two of them. The third put his rifle to his shoulder. Rasmussen had him covered and pulled the trigger, but there was just a click. The patrol man fired and the bullet pierced Rasmussen's chest.

Meanwhile Axelssen had got his revolver out and fired at the patrol man, who fled.

Although severely wounded, Rasmussen managed to get to the wire-netting fence at the end of the street, climb up, and roll over, keeping his face clear of the barbed wire. There was a ten-foot drop on the other side, but fortunately Rasmussen landed on a pile of firewood. Axelssen followed close behind. They had a contact who lived not far away, and attempted to get to his place, but Rasmussen collapsed when they were nearly there. With Axelssen supporting him, they managed to get a little further to where a delivery van was drawn up by the pavement. Axelssen had a word with the driver, who caught on at once. (With Rasmussen sagging at the knees, the situation was fairly obvious.) The van driver was a good chap, and without hesitation he helped Axelssen get Rasmussen in and they drove off.

Rasmussen came around in the van and asked the driver to take him to Midstuen Sanatorium, where the Swedish Red Cross had its hospital. He had to be carried in, the top half of him was covered with blood. A Norwegian doctor was sent for, but he could not cope with the situation. He gave Rasmussen a couple of injections, but flatly refused to bandage his wound. Instead, he sent for the hospital's head porter, whom he suspected of being in the Resistance Movement. The porter was one of my contacts, though neither Rasmussen nor Axelssen knew it, and he quickly secured an ambulance to drive Rasmussen to one of my hideouts in the suburbs. This was the house of a woman whose husband was in a concentration camp in Germany. She now lived alone with her children and had let us use her vacant rooms.

She had to get Rasmussen a doctor at once. This was easier said than done, but he came around sufficiently to understand and told them to get his brother-in-law, who was a doctor and lived in Sogn Garden City. The ambulance drove off at once and it wasn't long before it returned with Rasmussen's brother-in-law. The delays and all the handling had weakened Rasmussen so much that Mrs. Wideroe, in whose house he was, had to sit at his bedside for forty-eight hours, before it seemed that he would pull through.

Mrs. Wideroe had managed to get a message to me, so I arrived on the scene a couple of hours after Rasmussen reached her home. I was dreadfully sorry for Rasmussen, of course, but I had to think of other aspects of the case. What about clues? Had they left any that might lead the Gestapo and police to our hideout? What about the vandriver? Would he go to the police, who had offered a reward of 200,000 Crowns for information leading to the arrest of the two parachutists? The affair, of course, had caused a tremendous stir. The way the two had behaved had convinced the Gestapo and State Police that they must be people with special training.

I got the name of a reliable person in the firm which owned the van that had driven Rasmussen to hospital, and I went to see him that afternoon. By evening I was in touch with the man who had driven the van, a fellow called Ole Rothe. Having deposited Rasmussen, he had gone to his immediate boss, a man called Overby, and told him what had happened. Both Overby and Rothe had fought the Germans before and their sympathies were all with us. Overby at once reported Rothe as sick, and Rothe went into hiding till we should consider the danger over.

But what about the people at the hospital? Had they any idea where Rasmussen had been taken? And, even supposing the doctors considered this to come under their vow of secrecy, what couldn't the Gestapo get out of them?

I asked Rasmussen's brother-in-law how soon the patient could be moved, and was told that he ought to stay where he was for a week. It was too long to risk. We had to move him sooner than that. His brother-in-law understood. So two days later I arranged to transport him to a big house out at Vinderen. If we used an ambulance for the trip, it would be likely to be talked about, so again I had recourse to the head-porter at the hospital at Midstue. He was only too willing, and late that evening he drove out to Mrs. Wideroe's, we carried Rasmussen out on a stretcher, and took him off to the big house at Vinderen.

This had been a severe baptism for Axelssen, who was new to the game; but, nothing daunted, he went to the country south of Oslo, as planned, and carried out his duties very well.

Per Morland learned of the incident almost at once and he got busy. He put his contacts onto finding out how many Germans or State Police had been near the filling station in search of clues. Apparently quite a number of mysterious persons had been seen in the neighborhood and some might still be there, but nonetheless he went to the filling station in the afternoon, calmly got into the Chrysler, and drove it away with its arms and sabotage equipment intact.

With Rasmussen out of action and Axelssen in the country to the south, the Oslo Gang was no better off than before and it still needed reinforcements.

Early in January I had discussed the idea of another of the NORIC men in Norway coming back to Oslo, where he was accustomed to work. This was my old friend Martin Olsen, one of the reception party that had helped Haugland and me when we were parachuted down onto the Skrim plateau. One of the things Martin Olsen had done was to sink a German Cargo-boat down at Moss. He had simply swum a 100 yards through icy water in April, fixed a limpet charge to the boat's side, and that was that. At the beginning of March, Olsen was duly installed again in Oslo.

Friday, February 18, was a day of surprises. Hauge asked me to come with the Chrysler to one of our hideouts near Majorstue, and whom should I meet there but the head of our FO4 in London, Colonel Oen, who had come over via Stockholm to inspect the Home Forces in Occupied Norway. Talk about walking into the lion's jaws! And what a prize for the Gestapo! It seemed foolhardy to me, but that wasn't my affair. The following day I drove the Colonel up to Odal, northeast of the city. There, in the forest, he calmly inspected a parade of the Home Forces, all fully armed and equipped! What a sight that was!

I had long been in touch with the Colonel's family in Oslo, who had done a lot for us, including harboring radio-operators and other dangerous visitors.

With a couple of the Oslo Gang as his escort, Colonel Oen drove later to Kongsberg, where he and Hauge had a meeting with Professor Tronstad, the famous Norwegian scientist and expert on heavy water. We did not know then that the Gestapo were searching for the Chevrolet they drove—under the number it actually had at the time. We learned this later, when one of our "monitors" reported a conversation between the Gestapo in Drammen and the deputy sheriff in Hokksund, who reported having seen the wanted car going towards Kongsberg, and asked whether he should stop it on its way back.

At the beginning of March, after a fortnight's tour of inspection, Colonel Oen went back to Stockholm and London.

We were now very short of explosives. There was still no knowing when the war would be over. We could see that the final crash was coming shortly. Then in December there came the surprise Ardennes offensive and we had to carry on as before. London was informed of what we lacked, and the necessary material was dropped quickly north of Oslo.

Considering all the checks and controls the Germans now had, it was a real feat that we got all of these arms and equipment into the city without losing a thing. Then we had to store it somewhere. This meant finding a place for two tons of "plastic" high explosive. Our organization had dealt with just about everything, including storing arms and explosives, but not in such quantities. We had always been careful not to store arms or explosives in any of the flats where we lived or had our meetings.

We had got ourselves various stores, including a big shop on the outskirts that had closed down. We had also had a really good idea: We had made a number of tool chests like those of the Highway Department and other public bodies in Oslo that are spotted around the city. We put ours in various open places—preferably behind a fence and gate that could be locked—so we could be sure of privacy when we opened them. We had one, for example, in the big yard of a transport firm.

But where was I to put two tons of explosives? Eventually I was put in touch with the porter of a building where there was a big room available at the back. I told him I was supplying people who were in hiding, and that I had many sacks of potatoes that I must store as quickly as I could. (We had put all the plastic bags into ordinary potato sacks.)

The man agreed and watched with great interest when we stowed the sacks into his back room one evening. The following day, I had to go back to get a small supply. (I had naturally made sure that no one else could get into the room.) The porter appeared and asked eagerly if I could possibly let him have a sack of the potatoes. He must have thought me dreadfully mean when I refused. I wonder if he ever found out what really would have cooked if he'd heated any of those "potatoes." They were hot potatoes indeed!

CHAPTER XXV

Operation Cement-Mixer

Operation Cement-Mixer came at the beginning of March. We were to blow up the north-south railway lines in a thousand places simultaneously on the night of March 14th and no one was to start before eight o'clock in the evening. The question was how we could support the action in Oslo.

There was a meeting at the Holatex offices and I was later introduced to one of the chief railway executives. We decided to blow up the railways administration and office buildings, as that would cause endless confusion and hamstring coordination of track clearing and repairing. As the Germans had their transport office there, it would blow up as well; this would certainly hinder their troop transports. The whole point of the vast sabotage action was to prevent the Germans from pulling their divisions out of Norway and using them in their last counter-offensive on the Continent.

London approved the plan. I contacted Milorg's railway liaison man. He had already been in touch with the caretaker of the railway building, but meantime the caretaker had been arrested. We then had a word with the man's wife. We had no wish to make further difficulties for the poor woman, but she was only too anxious to do anything that would harm the Germans.

Recently we had been sent a number of very efficient officers from the War School in England. They were to take over various positions in

Milorg. One of these, Nordahl, was attached to us for this action, and he was keen for his first attempt at sabotage.

We got out paper and pencil and calculated how much explosive it would take to turn the railway building into a heap of rubble. We decided to make the attempt with four charges of 50 lbs. each.

We transported our explosives in ordinary suitcases; how were we to get so much there safely? Morland solved our problem. He had a friend in the fish trade, who had a warehouse just opposite the railway building, and this man agreed to let us put the suitcases there in advance of the action.

Carrying suitcases with such contents through the streets of Oslo after dark would have been fearfully risky; it would have been perilous even if we had used a car. As usual, the cheeky way was the safest. Morland drove down to the warehouse in broad daylight with four suitcases of explosives and two machine pistols with silencers. All this was placed against a wall behind some fish boxes. With so many explosives to handle, we thought it best to have another helper, and Milorg sent us one.

At nine o'clock that evening we assembled at the fish warehouse from our various parts of the city, hoping we had not attracted attention. Nordahl and two others were to place the charges and link them with the cordtex fuse. Pevik and I were to handle the guards.

At the back of the Railway Building was a small two-story building that housed several offices belonging to the State Railways and the caretaker's flat. A covered passage-way led from this small house to the Railway Building, a distance of about twenty-five feet. If we used this passage-way we hoped to take the guards by surprise.

The guard on the door sat in a sort of glass box just beside the main entrance. We had been given keys to all the doors we would have to pass through. There were said to be about ten Germans in the building—one and perhaps a Norwegian also in the glass box by the door, the others on the second floor and perhaps also in the attics.

Precisely at 9:30, Pevik and I left the fish warehouse. I walked a little way down the street and unscrewed the light bulbs at the entrance to the smaller railway building so our suitcases would not be too conspicuous when we lugged them across. There was considerable coming and going in the square all evening.

We reached the small building without incident and went in.

Morland and one of the others made a quick round of the offices to see if anyone was there and found two or three people working overtime. They were escorted at pistol point to the caretaker's flat. Pevik and I then went on down the passageway to the big building. We let ourselves in quietly and were soon at the glass compartment by the main door. In it sat a German with his pistol on the desk in front of him. He was completely taken by surprise. I twisted his arms behind his back and handcuffed him before he had time to say "cheep." Pevik kept him covered with a silenced machine-pistol.

Nordahl and his helpers now got busy with the charges. While they were occupied with this, the German recovered from the shock and got into a fine fury. He went for Pevik, kicking at him, and shouting as loud as he could to warn his companions on the floors above. It was a precarious situation. I went to see if Nordahl was ready, but he wasn't. When I got back to the main door, the German was still bellowing. Pevik called to me that we must make him quiet or people would hear him and give the alarm. We hesitated a moment for we would have preferred not to kill him, but he kept on shouting so we had no choice. A burst from the machine-pistol silenced him.

Five minutes later, the charges were all in place and linked with cordtex. While Pevik had been struggling with the German, I had locked the main door, so we now went back the way we had come. In the smaller building, Morland and his assistant joined us and, taking the later workers and the caretaker's wife with us, we walked out and mingled with the evening crowds. Then we made our various ways back home, with the satisfactory roar as the building collapsed still in our ears. There had been no way of warning the guards without endangering the whole enterprise. They had to be sacrificed.

The operation all but blocked the Germans' attempt to switch divisions from Norway to the Continent. A long time later, we heard that transport capacity had been reduced by seventy-five percent.

CHAPTER XXVI

An Eastern Trip

Our organization continued its usual intelligence work and one day in February London requested us to find out about the production of special diesel oil for U-boats at the refinery at Vallo, on the west side of Oslo Fjord. The Admiralty was interested in knowing where this oil was stored. I went to my best contact in Esso, who had no difficulty in providing the information London wanted, and I was able to send the following wireless message:

"Vallo does not produce diesel oil for U-Boats, only fuel oil for fishing boats, called SDKL. In Oslo Fjord are following stores of first-class diesel oil: Granerudstoa 2185 tons; Fagerstrand 1700 plus 1100 tons Heissöl, which corresponds to fuel oil No. 3."

On April 23 we sent a further message:

"From June 1944 to date Vallo received 18,000 tons of crude oil. Expects no more and has no stock. Result of refining 60 percent soler oil, rest unusable. Whole production goes to fishing fleet."

But Vallo was bombed and on April 26 we received the following message from London:

"Bombing of Vallo. Sufficient proof that Vallo oil products were used for military purposes. We are sorry for sufferings inflicted on civil population."

So, indeed, were we!

Throughout March I lived in a flat in a new building outside the city, which I sometimes shared with a man called Ringdal who was engaged in propaganda work. I was fascinated by this subject and we had many long talks about it and the assessment of public opinion and morale. The Resistance Movement's very existence depended, of course, upon the mood and will to resist of the ordinary man-in-the-street. It was on this endless number of sympathizers and helpers, in big ways and small, all over the country, that our work depended for its success. Ringdal worked with Manus, our specialist in propaganda now that Gram was gone, though ship sabotage was still his main concern. The British regarded psychological warfare as a crucial branch of the service of utmost importance in bolstering morale and resistance.

One day Ringdal did not turn up. He had been shot in an encounter with Germans in a flat in Bygdoy Alle.

At Easter time, Birger Rasmussen had so far recovered that we were able to start thinking of getting him across to Sweden. However, he was not supposed to move about much, so the overland route was obviously not for him. Fortunately, my friend at the Swedish Red Cross Hospital offered to drive him to Notteroy in a Swedish car, and he agreed to take another two men who also had to get to Sweden—people of some importance in our organization.

The next day I received alarming news: All three had been arrested by the Gestapo! Few things have shocked me more than that report. Now anything might happen, I told myself. I realized that, even if it were to be my last job, those three must be freed. What happened is perhaps best recounted by "Tore," who took part in it all and is now a professor at Oslo University.

"I hadn't intended to go away for Easter, 1945, but my plans were abruptly changed. It was a trip I shall never forget.

"The day before Maundy Thursday, I had been out and talked with a man who was to be 'exported.' I returned home and that evening, just before ten o'clock, the telephone rang. It was Sverre, as he always called himself when speaking to me [Jens Chr. Hauge]. He told me that they were to have a party and that I must join them. I was to come as I was and bring a parcel of food with me. I was to meet him in front of Frogner Church at a quarter past ten. I got there punctually and soon 'Ornulf' arrived. 'You're to go to Larvik,' he said. [Larvik is well south of Oslo on the fjord, south of Notteroy which is thirty miles from it.]

"I was accustomed to almost anything now, but this seemed a bit too much. There was no train until morning and auto travel was forbidden after ten o'clock. Then came the explanation: I would drive there with the 'State Police.' Then I learned the reason for this desperate action: Our export contact 'Harry' [the man who brought (Sonsteby) from Koster in January] had been captured at Notteroy and we were desperately concerned for three of our most important people whom he had had for export. If they had been arrested, they must be rescued, whatever the cost.

"We were first to search in Drammen, where Rolf had already gone to see what he could find out. I was to meet him there at twelve o'clock. Then, if necessary, we were to go on to Tonsberg and Larvik. I was to drive with two UK-men, No. 24 [Sonsteby] and Kristian [Arthur Pevik]. They had State Police identity cards and should be able to get through any control point. I had no such papers and was to pretend to be their prisoner. To make this look convincing, I was to be handcuffed. I was not to take actual part in freeing the three. If the UK-men needed help, they must get it from the local Milorg.

"No. 24 came with the car at eleven o'clock. The other UK-man, who was in the back, introduced himself. It was a good car. It had two generators fixed on behind, but they were for show only, for the car ran on gasoline.

"No. 24 said he thought it was silly to handcuff me and, as they were pretty uncomfortable, we dispensed with that idea. The cover story I had been given wasn't particularly convincing and none of us thought much of it. It would have taken a pretty dumb German to swallow it. Anyway, No. 24 was not much occupied with that problem. He had no intention that we should be taken alive.

"There was thick mist as we drove from Oslo. As we approached Drammen we slowed down, because we were ahead of time. There was a control post just outside the town. In the mist we barely saw the Germans' lights. The UK-men showed their papers, NORWEGISCHE STAATSPOLIZEI.

"The Germans looked at their papers and decided they were all right. I was referred to as their 'Gefangener.' There was a short chat; the

Germans told us that another time we must stop more quickly. We had gone beyond the sentries, and they had been on the point of firing at us. We explained that the fog had been blinding. Then there were two or three 'Heils' and we drove on.

"We were right on time as we pulled up outside the railway station in Drammen. The two UK-men sat waiting in the car a short distance away, while I kept watch outside the station building. There was a German patrol there and we mustn't arouse suspicion. Rolf didn't appear till half past twelve. I was standing in the shadow of the bridge keeping a lookout. I took him across to the car. He greeted No. 24. Rolf had been running around Drammen seeking information in vain. All his contacts were away or had left altogether, and he didn't know the normal reporting places for the couriers.

"We agreed that we should drive on to Tonsberg, leaving Rolf in Drammen to investigate further. The mist was thick on the road south and we strayed off the road once or twice. No. 24 drove all the time. Outside Holmestrand, a German car was stopped on the road and two Germans were waving their arms at us. We stopped. They were on their way to Drammen, but their generator was 'kaput.' They wanted us to tow them there. We had neither desire nor time for that; but since we were 'Stapo' we offered to drive one of them to the Ortskommandatur in Holmestrand. He thanked us and jumped in. Not much was said as we drove along, but when we put the German down at the Ortskommandatur's door in Holmestrand, he was very grateful.

"There was another control point at Nykirke. Seven or eight Germans came buzzing around us. No. 24 and his companion showed their identity cards and passes and the Germans became more chatty and amenable. It was all right because we were Stapo. The back seat was full of MPs and Mills bombs, so it was a good thing the Germans opened the front door and not the rear, when they looked inside. If they had opened the other, the Mills bombs would have rolled out and No. 24's identity card would scarcely have satisfied them then. They didn't ask about me. I got out and asked the Germans their advice. They warmly recommended the road via Horten. We thanked them for their advice and went by Horten.

"Between Horten and Tonsberg the ruts were so deep that the car began to bump on the ground, then all at once there was a clanking sound. We jumped out. It was the pipe between the generator and the engine. That didn't matter!

"We heaved sighs of relief. Now we could go home again. Tom got to the reporting places to try to get in touch with people. For two hours I raced about ringing the V-signal on people's bells and throwing pebbles at their windows in a vain attempt to find someone who knew what had happened at Notteroy.

"We had to go on to Larvik. There I managed to arouse the people at the report-station and they got me in touch with 'Tom'. Tom suggested that we go to our people who monitored the telephone. We managed to track down the head man there and he was able to tell us something.

"Harry and his sister had been arrested, but the three we were so concerned about had escaped through a window.

"The weather was fine and there were no controls on the way back. But we were stopped in Oslo itself by a patrol of Hirden's B.V. No. 24 showed our papers and all was well.

" 'Many control-points on the way in?' No. 24 asked.

" 'No. Not now.'

" 'Fine.'

"Even so we took the safer side-roads in to the city via Smestad and Vinderen. I got out at my home in Vinderen, tired and hungry. But I was no sooner in bed than Tor was on the telephone, asking me to meet him outside the stadium in ten minutes to report. There I met a smiling Rolf and told him the details. He was delighted and said he would go straight to the second man's parents and tell them their son was safe.

"Another thing I remember from the night's drive was that on the way back No. 24 was planning to rescue one of our women, 'Vera,' who had been arrested and put in Bredtveit. At the end, however, he was so tired that he was more than half inclined to give up the idea."

What had happened to the three, as I heard later, was this: Harry had been found by a control carrying arms and, of course, arrested. The three had then been surprised in Harry's house. However, they had been left alone for a short while and quickly opened the window, jumped through it, and took to the woods. Rasmussen became separated from the others but, though still convalescent, he managed to throw off the pursuit by hiding under leaves in a hollow. He lay there all night, and the next day fortunately ran into a Milorg man, who put him in touch with the export group again. The other two had also made contact with Milorg and in the evening all three were sailed across to Koster and from there reached Stromstad safely.

CHAPTER XXVII

Two Leaders Arrested

The Central Committee had an extensive network of contacts in every conceivable sphere; but the leader who impressed me most was Jens Chr. Hauge.

I remember how, when I came back from England in November, 1943, I had repeated strong criticism I had heard of certain government circles in London. Hauge refused to listen, saying that now we must all hold together. That was the right attitude. There was no room for wrangling. Hauge's great loyalty was a factor of real significance. He played a vital part in eliminating friction between the Norwegian government abroad and the Home Front. And what might not have happened if a man holding so many important threads in his hands had been activated by ignoble motives?

On Thursday, April 10, 1945, I had a shock when I went to Holatex for our daily meeting. Edvardsen (Jens Chr. Hauge) and Ornulf had been arrested. When the two did not turn up during the day, we were near panic. Two of the Home Front leaders were in the Nazis' clutches!

The following day I met two of Ornulf's closest collaborators. They believed the State Police were not aware of the role Hauge and Ornulf played. I talked of trying to rescue the two from Stapo HQ (where we knew they were) because if they were once transferred to the Gestapo,

CHAPTER XXVIII

We Get the Nazis' Archives

The end of April came. It could only be a matter of days. The Germans knew it and so did the Norwegian Nazis, for they began to burn their archives to remove all evidence of their rule of terror. The most important, where we were concerned, were the archives of the Nazi Police Department and the Nazi Department of Justice, and we had already made a few plans to make certain that they came into our hands. Now I was told that the time had come to take them.

It wasn't an easy job to carry out. I was given a contact in the Quisling Department of Justice to help me prepare the coup there. We would need a truck to cart all the files away and this was the snag, because that meant having to drive it up to the main entrance in Grubbe Street and letting it stand there only fifty or sixty yards from the entrance to Head Police Station in Moller Street. Milorg had put me in touch with the caretaker of the Police Department's building, who was to help plan the "theft" of the archives there.

We conferred and concluded that the only sensible thing to do would be to coordinate the two actions. We could use the big central courtyard and drive in from Akers Street. If we could overpower the guards, we ought to be able to work in relative security. Unfortunately, the guard system was a very efficient one. The outer door was kept locked. Behind was a shed used as a guardroom. One man patrolled outside the shed behind the door and another sat inside the shed with an alarm button beside his hand, which alarm rang bells in both departments and also in the police station at No. 19. Thus it would be impossible to accomplish everything in silence, unless we had the help of the guards. The situation was very tense, and our orders were that there must be no shooting or trouble.

Through the heads of our underground police department I got in touch with a good patriot among those stationed at No. 19. His name was Eivind Eriksen, and it was he who posted the guards in the two departments that week, so he was doubly important. I asked him to see if he could find two guards willing to help and disappear with us after the coup. Eriksen thought this would be easy, and promised me an answer at two o'clock the next afternoon. We agreed that our two "helpers" were not to be told the actual plan, because we didn't want them to be forced to give everything away, if caught.

For this big action, the Oslo Gang was reinforced by four people from Milorg, so there were eleven of us. I was to lead the group dealing with the Department of Justice and Martin Olsen was in charge of the men attending to the Police Department.

We got ourselves a nice big van and the resourceful Pipe Larsen found us name boards for it saying "Oslo Express Service," plus all the furniture mover's equipment we might need.

At six o'clock on the evening of May 2, I strolled up the gateway in Akers Street, gave the password "Martinsen," and was admitted by the patrolling sentry. Together we went to the shed where the other men sat.

I was now to brief the men, and they were on tenterhooks. For some reason I became fearfully nervous and couldn't get a word out. (I had never before had difficulty with my nerves. I had felt the tension and excitement before every action, as we all did, but once we had started I used to be perfectly calm). Now I stood there unable to utter a word. My mouth was dry and I made desperate attempts to moisten my lips. I began again and again, but couldn't get anything out. However, after a couple of minutes, my state improved and soon I was back to normal.

I told the three policemen that five of us were going to let ourselves into the Quisling Department of Justice, using the entrance in Grubbe Street, at 6:15 exactly. A quarter of an hour later, one of us would walk across the courtyard and come to the shed. One of the guards was to open the outer door, our man would signal to a van waiting at the corner, which would then drive in.

I went back to the gate in Akers Street and a little way down the street met one of the gang, now in police uniform, and one of the secretaries in the Department, Paul Stensholt, who was going to show us the important files in his department for us to take.

Two more of the gang (one in police uniform) were standing further down the street. As the door to the Department was in full view of the policemen on guard at No. 19, we had to be careful not to arouse suspicions. We went to the caretaker of the building and told him that we were police come to search the place because the resistance people had dangerous papers and propaganda material hidden in it. We pretended to be picked NS men. The caretaker, afraid for his own skin, was very obsequious and wanted to show us around. It was difficult to convince him that he had best disappear into his den to his family and stay there under guard.

Two of our group stayed in the caretaker's flat, while another and I made the rounds of the building. We found three of the staff working overtime, told them of the search we were making, and saw them down to the caretaker's flat. It was now six-thirty and my companion went across the courtyard to start the rest of the action. Meanwhile the departmental secretary showed me around, unlocking the more important doors with his own keys, and showing me where the most important files were. That done he left. We didn't want to involve outsiders if things should go wrong.

At six-thirty the furniture van drove into the courtyard, the back was opened, and the gang trooped into the Police Department. They found two men in the room with the telephone switchboard, our friend the caretaker, and a policeman.

They then divided into two groups so as to surprise a Nazi who was working at the State Police card index on the first floor. He was armed and must not be given an opportunity to fire a shot. It was all easy. The man was so nervous he couldn't get a word out, let alone do anything. It was a comfort to me that others could be like that too!

One of the gang in police uniforms was installed in the guardroom and our accomplice, who had been there earlier, was in charge of the switchboard. A couple of Milorg men were looking after the prisoners.

Any new arrivals were to be held up, brought in, and tied up.

During the next forty minutes we loaded two tons of files into the van. We had to take one safe weighing 700 kilos. Though we had strong arms and stretchers, it was impossible to *carry* it down the stairs, and we had to roll it all the way down. Its passage, I am afraid, furrowed holes that called for immediate repair, but that was not our concern.

We drove the van to the door of the Department of Justice building. All the files we wanted were now piled up in the corridor. It was obvious that the Nazis had already burned a certain amount, but we had got quite a lot of important stuff in the "Minister's" own room. We took about half a ton of files from this department.

The van group clambered in again, the back was closed, and the two guarding our prisoners were told that it was all over and they could release their victims. Aubert and I went out by the main gate and saw that it was shut properly behind us.

While we were doing this, three of the Milorg men had visited the home of the chief secretary of the department who had the keys to the big safe. With a pistol at his head, they persuaded him to hand the keys over and they were in our possession ten minutes later.

When the van was a few blocks away, we stopped to remove the name-boards of the Oslo Express, which everyone would be looking for, and drove on.

A while after we had gone, when all had been discovered, the caretaker of the Department of Justice building went across to ask when the relief was coming for the police who had been searching this building. These, he said, had gone, but they had told him to stay where he was till reinforcements came for a bigger search that was going to be made.

The alarm was given by the man who had been working on the card index. When he found himself free, he rushed out into the street shouting for help.

We had saved many important documents from destruction. They played a stellar part in the trials of our Nazis after the war and threw a lot of light on the arbitrary doings of the NS party during the war.

CHAPTER XXIX

The Liberation

In the afternoon of May 5 I took the elevator up to the Holatex offices, which were no longer Holatex but the HQ of the Central Committee of the Home Forces—now a free and open fact. I could still scarcely believe that the thing for which we had hoped so long had come about. Hitler's rule was broken. Norway would soon be free.

Hitler had committed suicide five days before and his successor, Admiral Dönitz, surrendered unconditionally two days later. The leaders of the Home Front were still uncertain about General Böhme and the Germans in Norway. Would they too surrender? The hated Reichskommissar Terboven was still in power and his power was considerable.

On Sunday, May 6, there was a rumor that the Germans in Norway had capitulated, but later in the day this proved to be premature. The following day, the surrender was a fact. Terboven had been dismissed and Dönitz had ordered General Böhme to surrender unconditionally at 21.10 hours.

I got out my battledress, and the owner of the flat where I was then staying and her daughter sewed on the shoulder flaps. My orders were to be ready for instant action and to be in continual touch with the rest of the Oslo Gang.

At one o'clock in the night of the 8th, Hauge told me to call up the other members of the Oslo Gang and meet him as soon as possible at 19 Moller Street. We were to be armed. I soon got hold of the other five. Our two piats were already in the luggage compartment of the car, so we were outside the police station before many minutes had passed. We met Hauge at 1:30 a. m. He told us that some of the Home Front leaders were at 19 Moller Street and that we must guard it. They had reason to fear that armed units of fanatical Nazis were going to attack the place.

We made them lock the doors of No. 19 from inside, and we closed the entrance gate. Then we sat up our two piats just outside the entrance, and the rest of us took up position with machine-pistols ready in Moller Street and neighboring Ploens Street. I had armed myself with a good stout Tommy-gun and now took one of the others to stop any car that might come along. The Nazis were said to be on their way into the city. As a further precaution I enlisted the help of the fire brigade and got them to roll a lot of logs that were stored further up the street to block the carriage-way. In this manner all streets leading into Moller Street were blocked. However, the Nazis never turned up and, after an hour or two, it became clear that it had been a false alarm.

I had taken the Mercedes Benz we were using and parked it just outside No. 19. My uniform, put on in such a hurry, was far from complete. Blouse and beret were all right, but below that I was wearing ordinary knickerbockers. I was more a figure of fun than one likely to inspire respect, and it wasn't till I brandished my Tommy-gun that people realized they must do what they were told.

Units of the Home Forces in Oslo arrived about two or three o'clock and relieved us of our guard duties, but a short while later—about four or five that morning—I had a very curious experience. I had to take the Swedish policeman, Harry Söderman, to the prison in Grubbe Street, where he was to meet Fehlis, the chief of the German security police. Fehlis arrived in a Mercedes sports car and offered to drive a couple of carloads of arms for us from his HQ in Victoria Terrace! And that was done. It was an extraordinary sensation finding oneself face to face with the notorious Fehlis. Yet it was he, I heard, who gave Harry Söderman power to go to Grini Prison and open its gates and let everyone out.

That morning Martin Olsen and I, now in full uniform, drove through the city. It was a remarkable experience, and I continually had to assure myself that it was real. The time was over when I had to go about with an innocent poker face calling myself Krogh or Fjeld or Berg, knowing that the Gestapo were hunting me. I could be myself and let everyone know that I was I—Gunnar Sonsteby. It was like being re-born on that glorious sunny day of Oslo's freedom.

There were still things to be done. The Oslo Gang had to have a headquarters. Hearing that "Minister" Blehr had fled from his home, I went to his house, knocked out a pane of glass in the front door and let myself in. There we established ourselves and there we lived comfortably till the Foreign Office took the house over and turned us out.

Rasmussen and Manus arrived from Sweden. Axelssen came in from the south. Diesen emerged unscathed from prison and there we all were, able to rejoice together that the strain of our years of sabotage and conspiracy was at an end.

In the days that followed we did all sorts of guard duty. Several of the NORIC men came in from the country and joined us.

Then Martin Olsen and I were summoned to the Police HQ. Would we, we were asked, act as Crown Prince Olav's escort and be answerable for his life, when he came back to Norway on May 13? There was nothing we would rather have done, of course, so the reinforced Oslo Gang became the Crown Prince's bodyguard. We also served as King Haakon's bodyguard when he came home on June 7.

In those hectic days, for all our rejoicing, Oslo was not the safest place. Norwegian Nazis and German Gestapo men had gone into hiding. They were all armed, and one could not discount the possibility of some desperate fanatic's reaction to the city's delirious joy.

One of the last things we had to do was to take Quisling from Moller Street to Akershus for his trial. At eight o'clock on the morning of August 19 we paraded in the courtyard of No. 19. Then there was our prisoner—the man we had hated and feared—powerless and helpless. We felt a little sorry for him. He fumbled with the blankets he had to take with him and dropped one of them. I felt that I wanted to help him pick it up, and I saw from my old friend Rivrud's face that he felt the same. Rivrud had spent the latter part of the war in a German concentration camp, but had survived. It was he who went in the car with Quisling. There was a sort of compassion in his gaze.

With a sense of liberation I boarded a boat for America and sailed away from it all that fall. Only then was I convinced that those years were over—that I could concentrate on the proper objective of all who are only twenty-seven years old: the future.

Epilogue . . .

My war time associate and friend Captain Gunnar F. T. Sonsteby, formerly of the Royal Norwegian Army, is a man of fine intelligence, high character and exceptional qualities as a leader.

He showed these qualities as central control officer and chief of operations in the Norwegian underground organization in which he was an active force from the time of the German occupation in 1940 until the end of the war.

He displayed sustained coolness and courage in leading a series of 17 attacks against German units and installations in the Oslo area from May to October 1944. These included (1) an attack on the German air depot at Korsvoll and the destruction of 44 Nazi aircraft; (2) with 2 helpers the destruction of a machine tool plant together with guns and machinery of the Kongsberg Arms Factory which was patrolled by 20 guards and protected by police dogs and land mines; (3) the invasion of German oil storage depots, destroying thousands of gallons of enemy oil.

In November of 1944, after a special course of instruction in England he returned to Norway as chief of all sabotage operations in the region of which Oslo was center. In this position he not only won recognition for his executive and administrative ability but also for his skill, daring and imagination in the planning and the execution of raids.

Sonsteby was the only Norwegian who was awarded the Norwegian War Cross with two bars—the highest award given by Norway during the war. On the return of the Royal Family in 1945 he was appointed Chief of the Royal Bodyguard. In recognition of his outstanding service, he was decorated by the British and the United States governments.

In Norway he is held in high regard for his patriotism, his loyalty and his personal character.

WILLIAM J. DONOVAN
Major General, U.S.A., Res.